30 Collaborative Books

for Your Class to Make and Share!

Easy Patterns & How-to's for Creating a Year's Worth of
Thematic Rhyming Books

by Mary Beth Spann

Weather Watch

I open my curtains,
and what do you guess?
Today's weather is _Sunny_
so this is how I'll dress:

Name _James_

Snowman Alive!

Yo, man! Snowman!
Frosty head-to-toe man!
I wish you were real, you know?
Then we could _go sledding_
here in the snow!

Name _Lee_

My Tree and Me

Each season I visit a special tree
to see how it changed and grew.
And the tree is not the only one...
each season I'm changing, too!

This _Summer_ season
my tree and I look like this:

Name _Katherine_

SCHOLASTIC
PROFESSIONAL BOOKS

New York ■ Toronto ■ London ■ Auckland ■ Sydney

Dedication

To my dear mentor, the late Dr. Aaron Lipton, who knew best how to champion each child's precious spirit. I will always love and admire you. I am trying hard to remember and live by all you taught me.

With love, to my special little girl, Francesca, who let me into her classroom so I might share my puppets, my stories, and especially my love of writing with her and her classmates. Thanks, sweetie.

With love, to my dad, Albert Spann, who read to me and took me to the library before I could read. To my sister, Colleen, who loves books almost as much as I love her. And to my sweet baby James and husband Frank, just because I love you both.

Acknowledgments

With special thanks to Becky Skrzypecki, first-grade teacher at Riley Avenue School, Calverton, New York, who generously allowed me to come into her class and test my collaborative book ideas with her students. Thanks to her terrific open door policy, parents like me are able to enjoy an important sense of connection to the classroom. If teachers everywhere followed her lead, we could change the face of education.

Thanks also to the wonderful, talented children in Mrs. Skrzypecki's first-grade class who cheerfully tested the ideas in this book. They taught me much more than I taught them.

Great appreciation and love to my friend and colleague Jane McGilloway, who helped inspire this book with her love of fun-filled writing projects and her dynamite ideas for book shapes. Thanks to Theresa Fitzgerald, Jan Pyk, and the talented staff of Boultinghouse & Boultinghouse who helped make this book come alive with art and design. And, as always, huge thanks to Scholastic editors Terry Cooper and Liza Charlesworth, who nudged me to give it a go, then supported me every step of the way.

Cover design by Jaime Lucero

Interior design by Ellen Matlach Hassell
for Boultinghouse & Boultinghouse, Inc.

Interior Illustrations by Jan Pyk and Manuel Rivera

Photos: pp. 5, 6, 8, 9: courtesy of Sandy Kolbo;
all remaining photos courtesy of Donnelly Marks

ISBN: 0-590-06542-4

Contents

The 30 Collaborative Books

Introduction

Welcome to the world of collaborative bookmaking!

This collection of fun-filled book-writing projects is guaranteed to engage beginning writers of every ability level. And you too will appreciate this easy-to-implement approach to bookmaking. Each and every selection is enjoyable to present and a breeze to manage. The book shapes and poetry selections were developed to match common themes that span the school year, but you can pick and choose to do them as you wish. They're so simple to execute and assemble, you can easily complete a book a week, confident in the knowledge that children are exercising their budding reading and writing skills.

Children love seeing their own library of original books grow. Each time they complete a book, they will bask in the realization that they are writing and reading as never before. Even family members appreciate getting in on the act as they share the finished books and offer important feedback. So what are you waiting for? Read on so you and your class can begin publishing today!

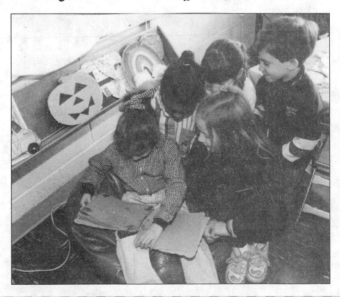

About the Collaborative Process in the Classroom

In a collaborative classroom project, each child contributes a unique, individual piece to the finished product. There are many reasons to include the collaborative process—especially the collaborative bookmaking process—in your classroom.

+ Collaborative books get everyone involved in the same effort; the books automatically generate a tremendous spirit of cooperation while still celebrating each child's unique contribution.

+ The collaboratives in this book are easy-to-facilitate writing projects. Because each child works on adding one page to the same book, you can feel focused as you help each writer personalize his or her page.

+ The completed collaborative book fosters respect for one another's work. Children get a chance to see the different ways their classmates responded to the same selection they were asked to complete.

+ Each of the 30 collaborative book selections is presented as a zippy, easy-to-learn rhyme. With only a couple of read-throughs, children feel confident knowing they can "read" the selection to themselves and to their friends and families.

+ The small shape-book format is charming to children and easy to tote home—just slip each book inside a self-closing plastic bag and it's ready to go!

+ Families love reading collaborative books. It gives them a window into their child's classroom—a way to see how their child and his or her classmates are progressing in writing. Plus, it offers them a feedback forum. (More on "family feedback" follows.)

How to Use This Book

This book contains 30 rhyming selections printed on 15 different-shape books (two selections per shape). The rhymes and shapes have been designed to enhance popular early elementary themes, but any selection can be completed at any time, just for fun!

The author, Mary Beth Spann (right), with first-grade teacher Becky Skrzypecki whose class made most of the collaborative books featured in these pages.

Each of the 30 collaborative selections includes a section that provides support for the step-by-step stages that follow. The steps are designed to help move the particular bookmaking process along smoothly from conceptualization to publication.

Prewriting Warm-up

This section offers simple discussion ideas to acquaint children with the topic at hand and to bridge the gap between what they know and what they will write. Here you set the stage for the writing to come.

Introducing the Selection

At this stage of the bookmaking process, children learn exactly what they will be expected to write about to help contribute to the collaborative book. Here you'll find specific ideas for introducing each selection as a reading/reciting activity. We suggest you first print each selection on sentence strips (for use with a pocket chart), chart pad paper, or the chalkboard. Then you can introduce the selection to the whole group at once. By offering children a blank space to fill in or an open-ended question to answer, the selections offer an easy-to-use framework for children's early writing attempts. (**Teaching Tip:** The blank space in the pocket chart selection can confuse children who don't realize that it stands for a word or words. You may want to fill the space with a sample response. Then encourage children to record original responses, rather than copying your sample.)

Writing Together

Located here are specific tips for making the most of children's writing efforts. For most book models it works best if children think of more than one response to complete the selection. That way, children begin to understand writing as a powerful medium that offers them choices.

It also can be helpful to provide children with sticky notes on which they will use developmental spelling skills to jot a rough draft of what they eventually will write on their book page. (Unlike other scrap papers, the sticky notes tend to stay put and don't get lost in the shuffle.) Then we suggest you meet briefly with each student to revise his or her efforts. As part of the editing process, you may want to have them recopy (or recopy for them) their polished versions on a second, different-colored sticky note.

It's important to stress to children that because this will be a published work designed for other people's eyes, their work must be edited and polished. Because the expected writing is kept to a minimum, even children with the most limited writing experience glide easily through this editing/recopying step.

Illustrating Pages

After children have finished writing, invite them to illustrate the poems. Be sure to have plenty of crayons and markers on hand. When their illustrations are complete, you might suggest that children "fill their pages with color" by using a crayon to add warm background shadings. This will make each page more colorful and distinct. (**Teaching Tip:** Caution children not to color too heavily over the print on the page.)

Follow-up Activity

Here you'll find hints, activities, and suggestions for keeping the learning alive when the book has been "put to bed." (That's publishing talk for *finished!*)

Best-Book Connection

We recommend one children's book hand-picked to enhance each selection's conceptual nuances. The suggested titles dovetail with and support the bookmaking effort.

The Step-by-Step Process to Publishing a Collaborative Book

To publish any one of the 30 collaborative book projects, just refer to the information about each selection presented in this book, then follow these simple steps:

1 Choose a shape book and selection.

2 Make enough photocopies of the page template so each child has one page.

3 Present the topic and selection to the class.

4 Have children use developmental spelling to record their thoughts on sticky notes (or take dictation from students who are not yet ready to write).

5 Help them edit their work and copy the edited version to the book page.

6 Have children illustrate their book pages, then cut them out.

7 Bind their pages between the matching book covers prepared from the reproducible template.

8 Read and share your finished publication.

Children reading their collaborative books.

Publishing Tips

These production tips will help your publication sparkle.

✚ Copy the book cover onto construction paper. To further strengthen the covers, make two copies for the front and the back of the book and glue these together. You may also use the cover page as a pattern and cut the shape from oak tag; add details with markers or paints. To make books extra-sturdy, bind a matching back cover to each book.

✚ You can keep your covers simple. Ask volunteers to add some color with crayons, paints, or markers. But for truly captivating covers, look for the Cover Design Ideas that appear with the introduction to each book.

✚ Consider copying the page templates onto drawing paper, trimmed to fit your copy machine, if necessary.

✚ Cut additional book pages from drawing paper to serve as follows:

- ■ a title page

- ■ a dedication page (complete with copyright information and your publishing house's name—we dubbed ours "Riley Avenue Press")

- ■ family feedback pages (to be placed in the back of the book) complete with an invitation for family members to offer their comments

- ■ an About the Authors and Illustrators page. Add a class photo (or a photocopy of one) along with a short write-up about children and their interests. Glue this page to the inside back cover of the book.

✤ Use a paper punch to punch holes in each page and the book covers. Look for guide circles for placement. Or, you can use an electric hole punch, which really makes the job easier. Reinforce each hole with a self-sticking loose-leaf hole reinforcement. After assembling the book pages in order, attach loose-leaf rings or thread ribbons, yarns, or pipe cleaners (twisted together to form rings) through these holes. Number the pages, if desired.

Suggestions for Sharing the Books

After your bookbinding is done, the fun's just begun! Here are some special ways for getting the most mileage out of your publications:

✤ Place the books in your class library. Allow children to read them as they do other books you make available. Of course, it's always wise to hold a discussion from time to time about the importance of caring for books, but children are usually careful with their own publications. If the books begin to show wear, add a bit more reinforcement or a fresh book cover. (**Teaching Tip:** This refurbishing process is a good job for family members who want to volunteer for your class from home.)

✤ Tuck the books in self-closing plastic bags to circulate home with students.

✤ Before the first book goes home, provide students with a take-home letter to the families describing the program and its benefits. (See the sample letter on the next page.)

✤ As the books travel back and forth, remember to check the "family feedback" pages from time to time. Comments from family members can offer you a real boost and can be very helpful.

✤ Hold a book fair and invite family members and other classes to view your collection.

The author shares a collaborative book with its creators.

✤ The book shapes and covers can be used to create individual books, too. Many of the selections can be copied more than once, thus allowing students to record more than one response (or you can just trim blank papers to fit behind the covers). Of course, the resulting individual books are not collaborative in nature. But if every child makes the same book model, the books can be grouped together on the same interactive bulletin-board writing center display. Children can then take a book down, read it, and replace it—once again appreciating their classmates' efforts.

✤ One great feature of the collaborative book pages is that each has a self-contained rhyme. At year's end you can disassemble each collaborative book and bind each student's pages together, thereby forming individual collections for students to keep and treasure.

No matter what kind of writing program you have in place, you will enjoy including these books in your writing curriculum. And you will be pleased with the writing that results. Let us know how the program turns out for you. We'd love to hear from you!

Sample Letter to Families

Dear Family:

Our class is working on an exciting project that involves all the students in creating a series of collaborative books. Each child will contribute one page to each book, featuring the same design and preprinted passage geared to a classroom theme (back to school, weather, and so on). Children complete their pages by adding their own words and illustrations. This bookmaking technique is especially effective because it automatically adjusts itself to each learner's level (instead of the other way around). Children who are not yet ready to write can dictate to the teacher and can contribute to the same book as children who are proficient writers. The rhyming, repetitive passages are fun for young children to read and complete.

Many of the books simply ask children to slot a word or phrase into a passage. More open-ended selections offer children the chance to write a bit more, if they are ready. Children will write a rough draft using the developmental spelling method (where they spell those letter sounds they hear), and they will also edit and polish their work for "publication." Each page has space for them to add an illustration.

When they share the completed books, children will learn to respect their own ideas as well as those of their classmates. Plus, as they take turns bringing the books home, children will have a chance to experience the added thrill of sharing the books with you, their families. Please read the passage that appears on each page with your child. Together you can experience the joy that reading and writing can bring.

The children and I expect that every family will be enthusiastic about the books. At the back of each book is a page for you to jot important "family feedback." We care what **you** think about our books!

Please let me know if you can lend a hand during our collaborative writing sessions, which will take place every Wednesday morning from 10:00 to 10:45.

Thanks you so much for your support!

Sincerely,

_____

Your Child's Teacher

The 30 Collaborative Books

Playful Penguin
by
Ms. Martin's class

Shopping Cart
by Ms. Martin's class

Lucky Rainbow
by
Ms. Martin's class

Tick-Tock Clock
by Ms. Martin's class

Busy Bus

This book in the shape of a school bus, complete with wheels that really spin, will whisk your class to fun-filled writing adventures. The first collaborative selection celebrates school itself, and the second selection focuses on transportation. Climb aboard and get rolling and writing!

COVER DESIGN IDEA

Cut the bus shape from yellow oak tag. Referring to the cover template, use a fine-line marker to add bus details. Color in the windows with black marker. Add real turnable wheels to the bus by using extra pieces of black oak tag and brass fasteners.

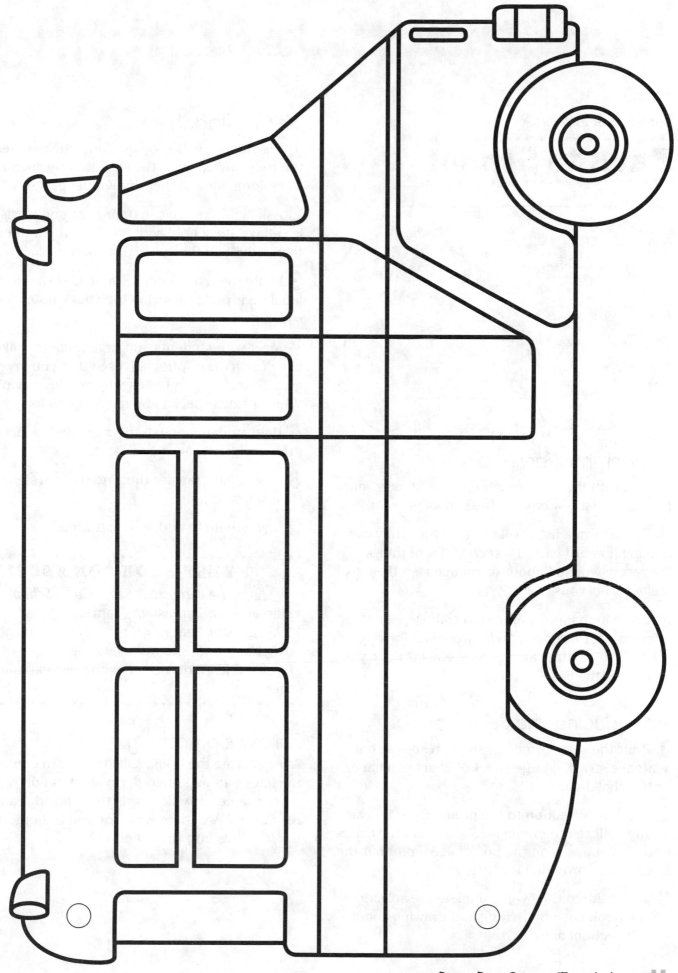

Busy Bus Cover Template   **13**

Busy Bus Selection A

Back to School

Prewriting Warm-up

1 Talk with the children about how "it feels" during those first few days of the school year.

2 Brainstorm a list of all the activities they were looking forward to and a second list of things they were worried about or that caused them to feel a bit nervous.

3 Invite individual children to elaborate on their offerings (for example, "Why were you looking forward to painting at the easel, Kaela? Have you worked at the easel before?").

Introducing the Selection

1 Print the selection and sample response onto sentence strips, a large sheet of chart pad paper, or the chalkboard.

2 Read the selection to the group. Read it again, asking children to chime in. Show them the selection as it appears on the book page. Point out the blank space provided for their responses.

3 Tell children they will complete the selection on the book page by writing and drawing about a favorite school activity.

Writing Together

1 Distribute the book pages and sticky notes for the rough draft. Read the selection through again as children look at their individual pages.

2 Ask children to close their eyes and to visualize a favorite school activity. Have them draw that activity in the space provided.

3 Invite them to use developmental spelling to label their pictures, using the sticky notes for a rough draft.

4 Meet with students and urge them to make use of rich descriptions. ("I see that you love gym class. Can you tell us why you love gym? What is extra-special about gym class for you?")

5 Help students polish their spelling, punctuation, and grammar.

6 Have them transfer their revised versions to their book pages.

7 Invite them to add an illustration.

BEST-BOOK CONNECTION

The Berenstain Bears Go to School by Stan and Jan Berenstain (Random House, 1978). Sister Bear is apprehensive about going to school, until she discovers the variety of fun-filled learning activities she will experience there.

Follow-up Activity

After sharing the book, ask children to consider the information gathered. Do most children prefer the same activities, or is there a wide range of responses? Are there ways for you to fit more of the favorites into the schedule?

Back to School

School! School! Here we come.
Lots to learn and so much fun.
Working, playing all day through,
and here's my favorite thing to do:

Name _____

Busy Bus Selection A: Page Template

Busy Bus Selection B

Traveling to School

Prewriting Warm-up

1 Ask children to brainstorm a list of ways we move from place to place. Tell children that cars, airplanes, trains, bicycles—and even feet—are known as "transportation."

2 Have them think to themselves and then count on their fingers the number of different vehicles they have used to travel about.

3 After sharing their vehicle experiences, ask them to take turns pantomiming other ways they might travel *without* a vehicle.

4 Ask them to raise their hands if they have ever ridden on a yellow school bus. Invite discussion about their bus-riding experiences.

Introducing the Selection

1 Print the selection and sample response onto sentence strips, a large sheet of chart pad paper, or the chalkboard.

2 Read the selection to the group. Read it again, asking children to chime in. Show them the selection as it appears on the book page. Point out the blank space provided for their responses.

3 Tell children they will complete the selection on the book page by writing and drawing about ways they travel to school.

Writing Together

1 Distribute the book pages and sticky notes for the rough draft. Read the selection through again as children look at their individual pages.

2 Ask children to close their eyes and try to visualize how they traveled to school that day. (**Teaching Tip:** If all children travel to school using the same mode of transportation, brainstorm a list of verbs related to that mode. For example, if all children ride a bus, generate bus-related transportation words such as *bounced, bumped, jiggled,* and so on.)

3 Have children draw themselves traveling to school in the space provided.

4 Invite them to use developmental spelling to label their pictures.

5 Meet with each student and foster the use of strong verbs and adverbs that will help to paint vivid pictures. Refer to any lists you have generated together. ("I see you are telling us you walked to school. Did you walk quickly or slowly? Did you run sometimes? Did you drag your feet? Use words to help me see how you walked.")

6 Help students polish their spelling, punctuation, and grammar.

7 Have them transfer their revised versions to their book pages.

BEST-BOOK CONNECTION
This Is the Way We Go to School by Edith Baer (Scholastic, 1990). A showcase of all the different ways children around the world get to school.

Follow-up Activity
Make a graph showing how many children walked or used different modes of transportation.

Traveling to School

Traveling to school every day,
lots of ways to go:
walking, rolling, hopping, riding,
moving fast or slow.

Today I _____ to school.

Name _____

Friendly Tree

This charming tree-shaped book may be shared any time of the year. Young scientists can use Selection A as a framework for keeping a nature journal. Selection B invites them to explore the branches of their family tree. Why not grow your own tree book today?

COVER DESIGN IDEA

On brown oak tag covers, use sponged-on paints to represent the tree at different seasons: pink and white for spring blossoms; green for summer leaves; orange, green, and yellow for the autumn leaves; and white for the snowy winter tree. Add bark lines with marker.

Friendly Tree Cover Template

Friendly Tree Selection A

My Tree and Me

Prewriting Warm-up

1 Ask children if any of them ever kept a tree journal (a popular early childhood activity). Have them describe what, if any, changes they noticed about their trees over time.

2 Make plans to have children "adopt" and observe a tree at school or at home.

3 Talk about the current season in your locale and how people outdoors dress for that season. Discuss how the trees are "dressed."

Introducing the Selection

1 Print the selection and sample response onto sentence strips, a large sheet of chart pad paper, or the chalkboard.

2 Read the selection to the group. Read it again, asking children to chime in. Show them the selection as it appears on the book page. Point out the blank space provided for their responses.

3 Tell children they will complete the selection on the book page by first decorating the tree to resemble the tree they observed, then decorating

the body outline to resemble themselves, and finally filling in the blank space with the name of the current season.

Writing Together

1 Distribute the book pages and sticky notes for the rough draft. Read the selection through again as children look at their individual pages.

2 Ask children to close their eyes and to visualize the tree they observed. Guide them to remember the tree's colors and how the leaves and branches looked. Also guide them to recall the colors and kinds of clothes they wore outside. Then have them use art supplies to complete the tree and the body outline.

3 Invite them to use developmental spelling to write the name of the season and to label their pictures.

4 Meet with students and encourage them to use as many specific labels for the tree and the clothing as possible. ("James, you say you 'wore a lot of clothes.' Let's name some of the autumn clothing items you wore, such as your striped hat and green jacket, so we can get a good picture of you dressed for the season.")

5 Help them polish their spelling, grammar, and punctuation.

6 Have them transfer their revised versions to their book pages.

BEST-BOOK CONNECTION
The Seasons of Arnold's Apple Tree by Gail Gibbons (Harcourt Brace Jovanovich, 1984). This story follows Arnold and his favorite tree through four seasons of activities.

Follow-up Activity
Make a series of "tree" books created at different times throughout the year.

My Tree and Me

Each season I visit a special tree
to see how it changed and grew.
And the tree is not the only one . . .
each season I'm changing, too!

This _____ season
my tree and I look like this.

Name _____

My Family Tree

My Family Tree

A family grows just like a tree
with branches large and small.
Count the folks on my family tree.
There are 3 members in all.

Name José

Prewriting Warm-up

1 Ask volunteers to try and define what is meant by the various titles of family members (for example, mother, father, brother, sister, grandmother, grandfather, uncle, aunt, cousin).

2 Talk with children about what is meant by a family tree. Ask them to go home and discover if they have their own family tree recorded in a book.

Introducing the Selection

1 Print the selection and sample response onto sentence strips, a large sheet of chart pad paper, or the chalkboard.

2 Read the selection to the group. Read it again, asking children to chime in. Show them the selection as it appears on the book page. Point out the blank space provided for their responses.

3 Tell children they will complete the selection on the book page by using the leaf shape to trace one leaf onto the tree for each family member, and then filling in the blank space with the total number of family members represented on their tree.

Writing Together

1 Distribute the book pages and sticky notes for the rough draft. Read the selection through again as children look at their individual pages.

2 Ask children to close their eyes and try to think of family members who are most special and important to them.

3 Show children how to cut out the leaf stencil and trace one leaf per family member onto their trees.

4 Children should then use developmental spelling to record important family members' names on the rough draft sticky notes.

5 Meet with each student to help polish spelling.

6 Ask children to copy the edited names onto the book pages, one name per leaf. They can then record the total number of family members in the space provided.

BEST-BOOK CONNECTION

Amelia Bedelia's Family Album by Peggy Parish (Greenwillow, 1988). Amelia Bedelia looks through her family album to decide whom she should invite to a party in her honor.

Follow-up Activity

Have children construct a matrix showing all the common family labels that apply to them (for example, daughter, sister, niece, cousin). Down the left-hand side of a large piece of chart pad paper, list children's names. Draw vertical lines separating the paper into a grid and then, across the top of the paper, note the family labels. Have children each place check marks next to their names indicating the labels that apply to them.

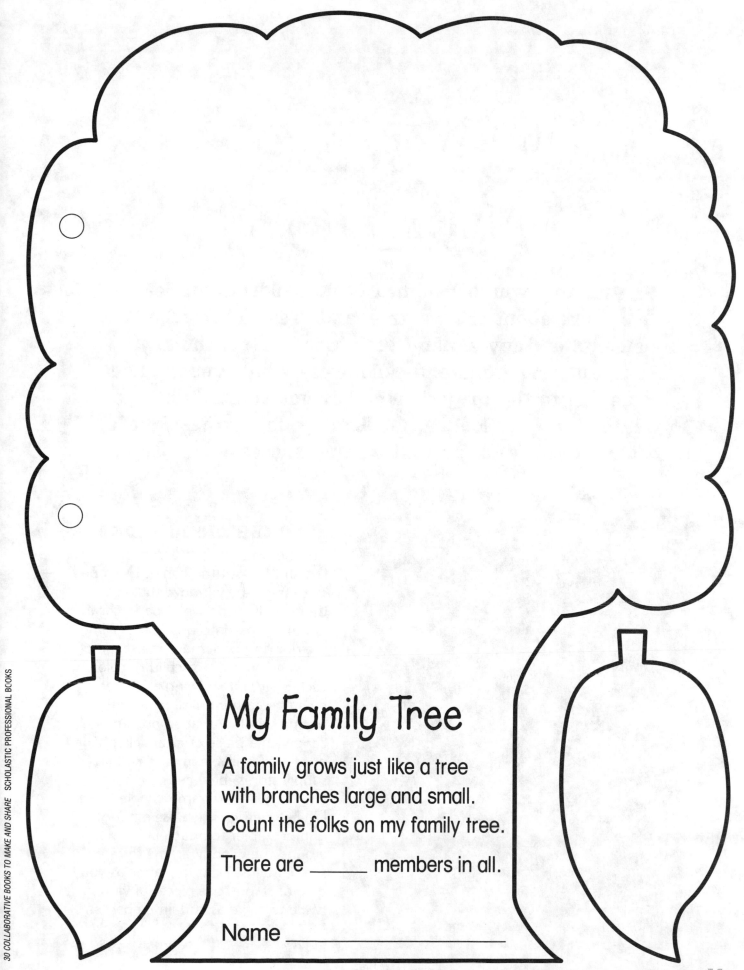

My Family Tree

A family grows just like a tree
with branches large and small.
Count the folks on my family tree.

There are _____ members in all.

Name _____

Friendly Tree Selection B: Page Template

Weather Window

With this window-shaped book, children will learn more about the weather and dressing for the elements as they expand their weather vocabulary. Real fabric curtains and cellophane windowpanes add some fun to the project. Whether you're studying the weather, or just looking for a rainy day project, these books are sure to forecast writing success!

COVER DESIGN IDEA

Cut the window frame from black oak tag and cut out the panes. Use a pencil to trace the window outline and the pane lines on white paper, dividing this paper into quadrants. Trim the drawing paper into the shape of the window. Invite a child to color each quadrant showing a different type of weather (or all rain for the second window-shaped book model). Sandwich a piece of clear cellophane or Mylar (available in craft and art supply stores) between the drawing and the window frame. Staple these layers together. Then use a hot-glue gun or stapler to attach fabric scraps around the window frame to represent curtains. Pleat the fabric as you glue or staple. Use pieces of yarn or twine to serve as curtain tie-backs.

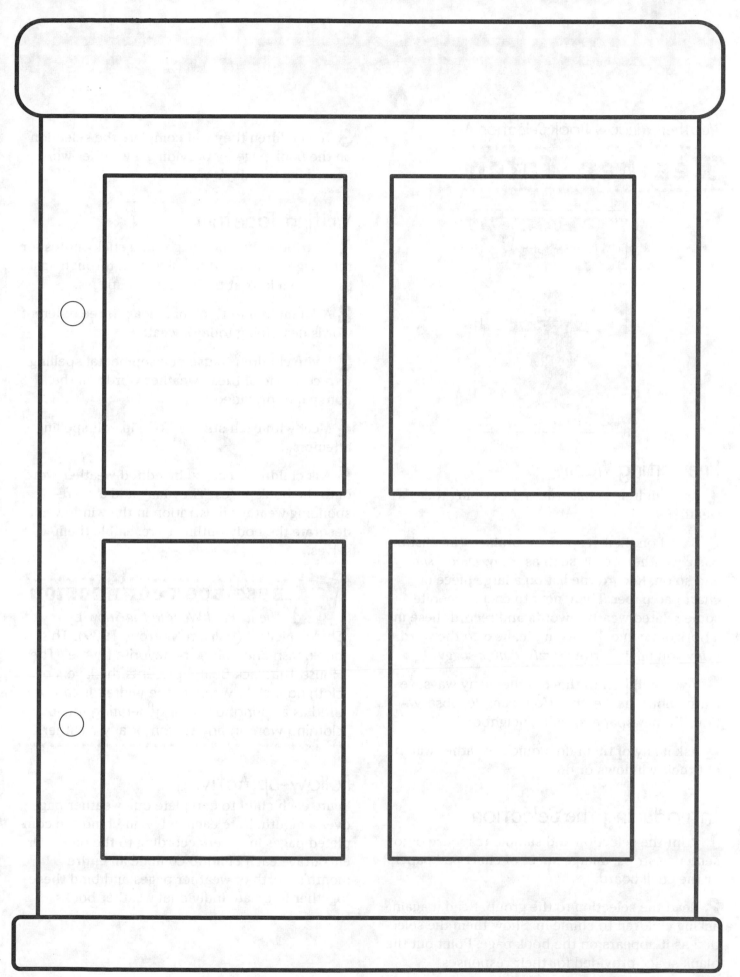

Weather Window Cover Template

Weather Window Book Selection A

Weather Watch

Prewriting Warm-up

1 Ask children to take turns describing today's weather.

2 Based on their responses, brainstorm a list of basic weather words such as *rainy, windy, snowy,* and so on. Record the list on a large piece of chart pad paper. Then, next to each, generate some related weather words and record these in a horizontal line. For example, next to the word *rainy* you might write *drizzly, damp, soggy.*

3 Invite children to think of the many ways we learn about the weather (for example, observation, TV, newspapers, radio, neighbors).

4 Ask if any of them do a quick "weather watch" out their windows or doors.

Introducing the Selection

1 Print the selection and sample response onto sentence strips, a large sheet of chart pad paper, or the chalkboard.

2 Read the selection to the group. Read it again, asking children to chime in. Show them the selection as it appears on the book page. Point out the blank space provided for their responses.

3 Tell children they will complete the selection on the book page by providing a weather word describing this day's weather.

Writing Together

1 Distribute the book pages and sticky notes for the rough draft. Read the selection through again as children look at their individual pages.

2 Ask children to think of at least three different words describing today's weather.

3 Invite children to use developmental spelling to record one of these weather words on the note paper provided.

4 Meet with each student to help edit spelling attempts.

5 Ask children to copy the edited weather word onto the book pages. They may add a corresponding weather illustration in the window and decorate the body outline to resemble themselves.

BEST-BOOK CONNECTION

The Jacket I Wear in the Snow by Shirley Neitzel (William Morrow, 1989). This book, fashioned after the favorite rhyme "The House That Jack Built," presents the layers of clothing a child wears in the winter. It can be used as a springboard for generating lists of clothing worn in any season or any weather.

Follow-up Activity

Invite each child to complete one weather page over a month. Date each entry and bind the completed pages in order according to the dates. Or encourage each child to compile an entire month's worth of weather pages and bind these together to create individual weather books.

Weather Watch

I open my curtains,
and what do you guess?

Today's weather is _____,
so this is how I'll dress:

Name _____

Rainy Rhythms

Prewriting Warm-up

1 Ask children to take turns telling how they feel when it rains.

2 Then ask children to make a list of rainy day activities they enjoy.

3 Tell the class that they are going to be making a book about what they can do when it rains.

Introducing the Selection

1 Print the selection and sample response onto sentence strips, a large sheet of chart pad paper, or the chalkboard.

2 Read the selection to the group. Read it again, asking children to chime in. Show them the selection as it appears on the book page. Point out the blank space provided for their responses.

3 Tell children they will complete the selection on the book page by telling what they like to do while listening to the rain.

Writing Together

1 Distribute the book pages and sticky notes for the rough draft. Read the selection through again as children look at their individual pages.

2 Ask them to think of at least three different things they like to do indoors on a rainy day.

3 Invite children to use developmental spelling to record one of these activities on the rough draft paper provided.

4 Meet with students so you can encourage them to be as detailed as possible about the activity they decided on. ("Freddy, I can see you like to play games. Can you tell us the name of your favorite game?")

5 Help them edit their spelling, punctuation, and grammar.

6 Ask children to copy their edited sentence ending onto the book pages. Then they can each draw a picture showing rain in the window and a picture of themselves doing the activity described.

BEST-BOOK CONNECTION
Peter Spier's Rain by Peter Spier (Doubleday, 1982). This wordless picture book presents a detailed account of two children's adventures on a rainy day.

Follow-up Activity
Distribute rhythm instruments and have children beat the poem's rhythm as you recite the selection. Then invite children to tell about an outdoor rainy day activity they each enjoy.

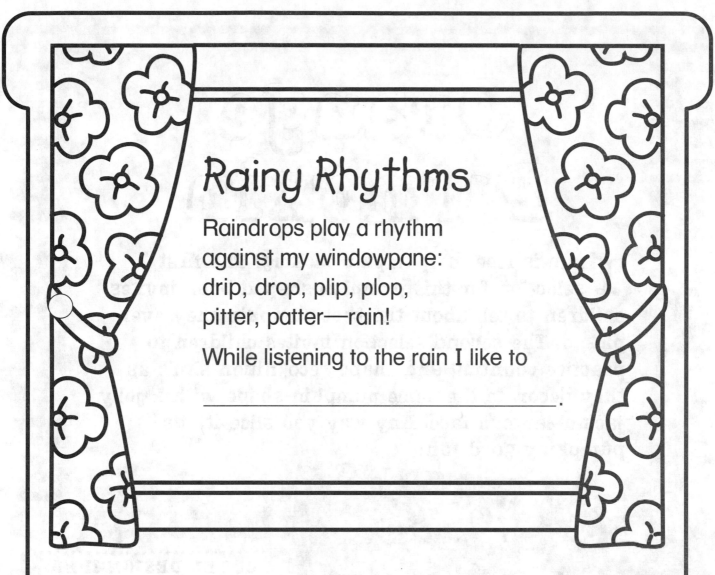

Rainy Rhythms

Raindrops play a rhythm
against my windowpane:
drip, drop, plip, plop,
pitter, patter—rain!

While listening to the rain I like to

_____.

Name _____

Orange Pumpkin

Time is ripe for pumpkin picking! The first selection for this pumpkin-shaped book invites children to tell about the best pumpkin they ever picked. The second selection invites children to practice counting and shape recognition skills as they decorate the same pumpkin shape with a jolly jack-o'-lantern face. Any way you slice it, it's pumpkiny good fun!

COVER DESIGN IDEA

Cut covers from orange construction paper or oak tag. Dip an old toothbrush in white paint and splatter it to create pumpkin bumps. Referring to the cover pattern, use a fine-line marker to create pumpkin crease lines. Add tiny dots with the marker to simulate imperfections and shadings along the top and left-hand edge of the shape. Cut three pumpkin leaf shapes from green oak tag or construction paper. Staple or glue these to a small piece of brown raffia. Staple a raffia "vine" to the pumpkin stem. Darken stem with marker.

For Selection B, cut a cover from fluorescent orange oak tag. Cut geometric shapes from black oak tag. Glue these to the pumpkin to make a smiling face. Referring to the cover pattern, use a fine-line marker to create pumpkin crease lines.

Orange Pumpkin Cover Template   **31**

Pumpkin Picking

Pumpkin Picking

I picked an orange pumpkin
right off of the vine.

It's as big as a *elephant*
and it's mine, all mine!

Name *Alexander*

Prewriting Warm-up

1 Invite children to talk about times they picked a real pumpkin from a farm field. Encourage them to tell how a pumpkin grows and what the farm field looks like. Ask if any children have ever chosen a pumpkin from a farm stand or grocery store. If possible, have a real pumpkin on hand.

2 Ask children to talk about what characteristics they look for and what to avoid when picking a pumpkin. List these on a piece of chart paper divided into two columns labeled "What to Look for When Picking a Pumpkin," and "What to Avoid When Picking a Pumpkin."

Introducing the Selection

1 Print the selection and sample response onto sentence strips, a large sheet of chart pad paper, or the chalkboard.

2 Read the selection to the group. Read it again, asking children to chime in. Show them the selection as it appears on the book page. Point out the blank space provided for their responses.

3 Tell children they will complete the selection on the book page by putting in the blank space a word (simile) that will tell how big their pumpkin was.

Writing Together

1 Distribute the book pages and sticky notes for the rough draft. Read the selection through again as children look at their individual pages.

2 Ask them to think of at least three different words they could put in the blank space so their selection makes sense.

3 Invite children to use developmental spelling to record one of these words on the note paper provided.

4 Help each student be as specific as possible while attempting to develop a simile. ("I see you say here that your pumpkin is as big as a 'ball.' Can you tell us what kind of a ball you mean?")

5 Help them edit their spelling, punctuation, and grammar.

6 Ask children to copy the edited simile onto the book pages. They can then draw pictures of themselves picking their pumpkins.

 BEST-BOOK CONNECTION
Big Pumpkin by Erica Silverman (Scholastic, 1993). A witch grows a pumpkin so huge she can pick it only with the help of some ghoulish friends.

Follow-up Activity

Visit a pumpkin patch and try to locate the largest and smallest pumpkin.

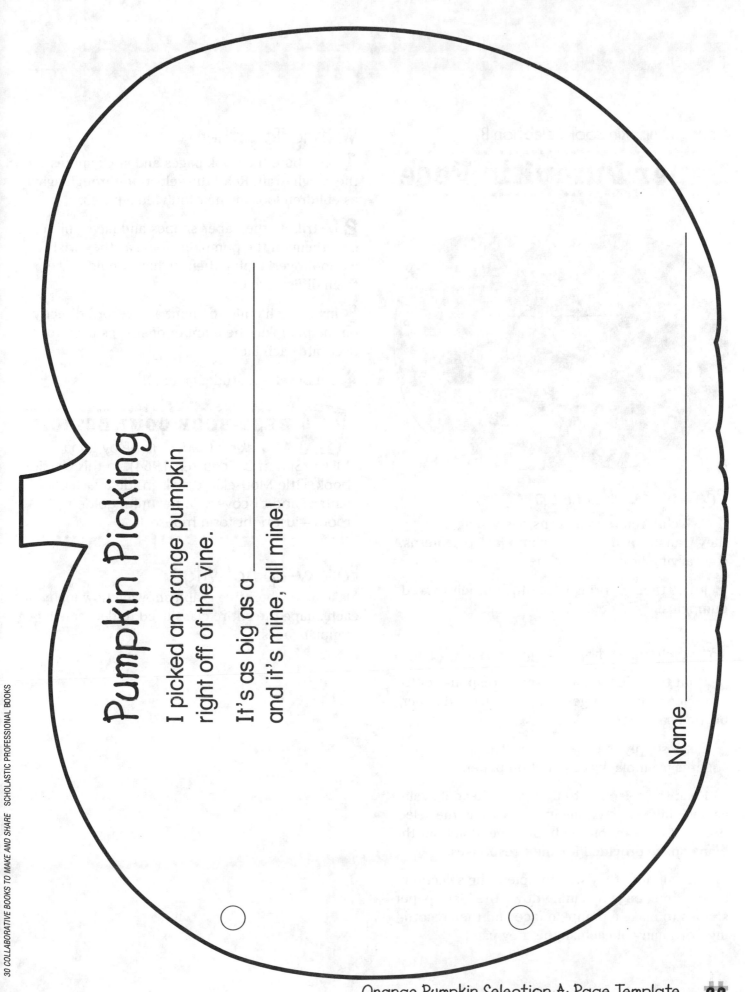

Pumpkin Picking

I picked an orange pumpkin
right off of the vine.

It's as big as a _____
and it's mine, all mine!

Name _____

Orange Pumpkin Book Selection B

Paper Pumpkin Face

Paper Pumpkin Face

I cut out a paper pumpkin, then added on a face.
I used 2 circle(s), 5 triangle(s), and 1 square(s).
In all, I used 8 shapes!

Name Aoi

Prewriting Warm-up

1 Ask children to take turns describing how they transformed pumpkins into jack-o'-lanterns. (by carving or decorating them)

2 Invite them to bring in photos of their carved pumpkins.

Introducing the Selection

1 Print the selection and sample response onto sentence strips, a large sheet of chart pad paper, or the chalkboard.

2 Cut a supply of paper circles, triangles, and squares from black construction paper.

3 Read the selection to the group. Read it again, asking children to chime in. Show them the selection as it appears on the book page. Point out the blank space provided for their responses.

4 Tell children they will complete the selection on the book page by gluing down the black paper shapes to make a pumpkin face and then recording how many of each shape they used.

Writing Together

1 Distribute the book pages and sticky notes for the rough draft. Read the selection through again as children look at their individual pages.

2 Distribute the paper shapes and have children glue them on the pumpkin shape as they wish without overlapping them (which would make them difficult to count).

3 Invite each child to count and record directly on the pumpkin the number of shapes used to decorate each face.

4 Double-check students' math.

 BEST-BOOK CONNECTION
Mousekin's Golden House by Edna Miller (Simon & Schuster, 1964). In this classic book, little Mousekin crawls inside a jack-o'-lantern and discovers "a beautiful golden room—just right for a mouse."

Follow-up Activity

Make a collaborative graph showing how many of each shape the entire class used to decorate its pumpkin faces.

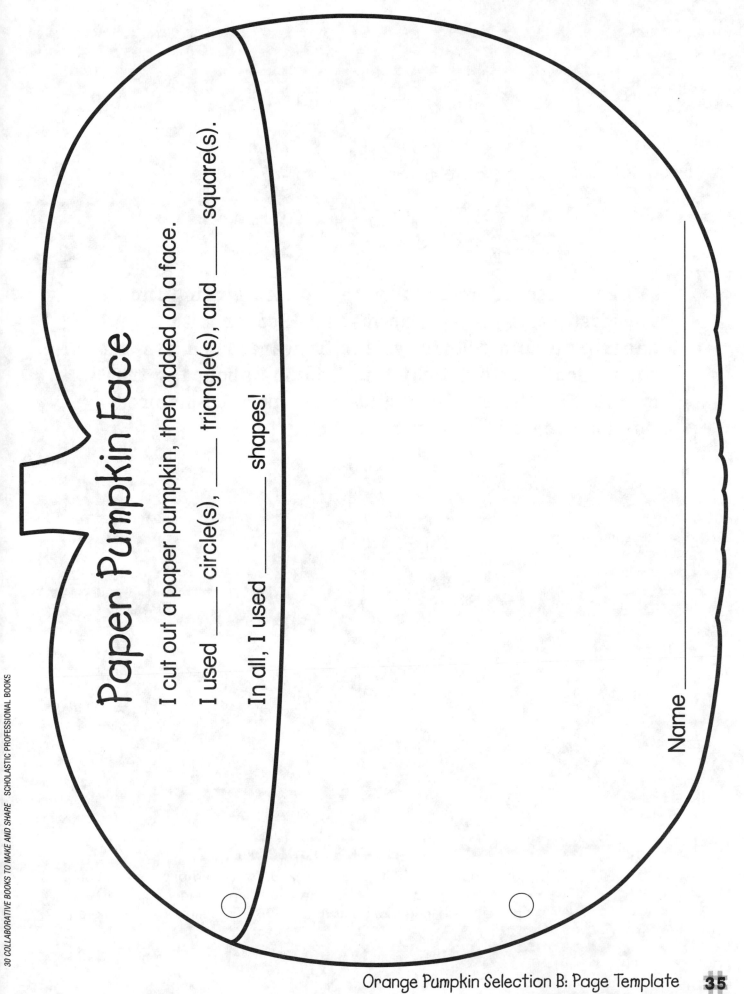

Paper Pumpkin Face

I cut out a paper pumpkin, then added on a face.

I used _____ circle(s), _____ triangle(s), and _____ square(s).

In all, I used _____ shapes!

Name _____

Pretty Placemat

Time to serve up some warm hearted writing fun! First, set a pretty placemat book cover with a real paper plate and colorful plastic flatware. Then use the book selections to get children thinking about the true meaning of Thanksgiving and to collect child-inspired tips for good table manners. Delicious!

COVER DESIGN IDEA

Use a hot-glue gun to attach a real dessert-sized paper plate, colorful plastic flatware, and construction paper dinner napkin to a placemat-shaped cover cut from brown- or cream-colored oak tag.

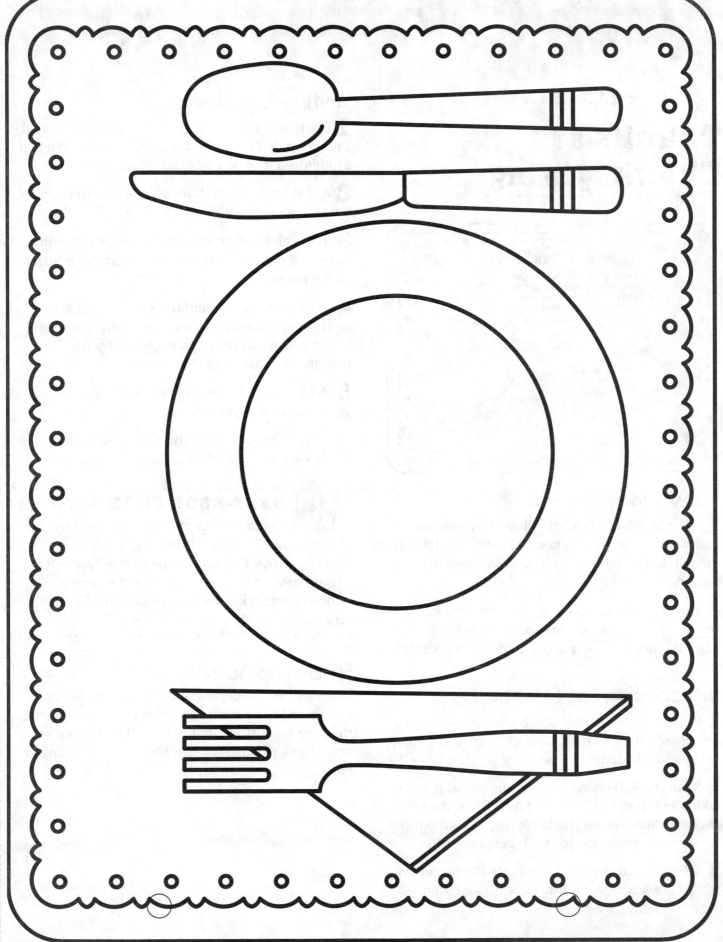

Pretty Placemat Cover Template

Thanks at Thanksgiving

Thanks at Thanksgiving

I think of sunshine, clear and bright.
I think of stars, twinkling at night.
I think of friends, family, and more—
I have so much to be thankful for!

I'm especially thankful for Max My cat

Name Alexandra

Prewriting Warm-up

1 Ask children to describe how they celebrate Thanksgiving at their house. Ask them to tell why we celebrate Thanksgiving. Encourage many responses.

2 Talk with children about the first Thanksgiving. Share books on the topic (See the Best-Book Connection for a recommended book title).

Introducing the Selection

1 Print the selection and sample response onto sentence strips, a large sheet of chart pad paper, or the chalkboard.

2 Read the selection to the group. Read it again, asking children to chime in. Show them the selection as it appears on the book page. Point out the blank space provided for their responses.

3 Tell children they will complete the selection on the book page by writing about something they are thankful for.

Writing Together

1 Distribute the book pages and sticky notes for the rough draft. Read the selection through again as children look at their individual pages.

2 Ask them to each think of at least three different things they are thankful for.

3 Invite children to use developmental spelling to record one of these ideas on their rough draft sticky notes.

4 Help students expand their ideas. Ask students who are ready to add the word "because" to their ideas so they can explain why they are thankful for whatever they chose.

5 Help students edit their work for spelling, grammar, and punctuation.

6 Ask children to copy the edited passage onto the book pages and then add an illustration.

BEST-BOOK CONNECTION

Thanksgiving at the Tappletons' by Eileen Spinelli (Addison-Wesley, 1982). Children love this funny tale of the Tappletons' Thanksgiving mishaps. Despite the family's holiday setbacks, the true meaning of Thanksgiving shines through for them all.

Follow-up Activity

Make additional copies of the poem for family members to complete, so children can learn what they are most thankful for. Bind these into a separate book titled *What Our Families Are Thankful For.*

Thanks at Thanksgiving

I think of sunshine, clear and bright.
I think of stars, twinkling at night.
I think of friends, family, and more—
I have so much to be thankful for!

I'm especially thankful for _____ .

Name _____

Mind Your Manners

Mind Your Manners

Grown-ups know a lot of rules
for eating at the table.
Here's one I try to keep in mind:

Chew with your mouth closed!

Now, see if you are able.

Name __Christopher__

Prewriting Warm-up

1 Ask children to tell what is meant by the saying, "Mind your manners."

2 Invite children to share any rules they have to follow to have good manners. Ask: Are all the rules about manners the same everywhere you go? From this discussion help children conclude that rules about manners can vary from family to famil, and from setting to setting.

Introducing the Selection

1 Print the selection and sample response onto sentence strips, a large sheet of chart pad paper, or the chalkboard.

2 Read the selection to the group. Read it again, asking children to chime in. Show them the selection as it appears on the book page. Point out the blank space provided for their responses.

3 Tell children they will complete the selection on the book page by providing a rule they know about good manners at the table.

Writing Together

1 Distribute the book pages and sticky notes for the rough draft. Read the selection through again as children look at their individual pages.

2 Ask them to think of at least three different rules to follow at the table.

3 Invite children to use developmental spelling to record one of these rules on the note paper provided.

4 Meet with each student to review his or her rule and to make sure it applies to manners. ("Well, Katie, it is a good idea to eat your vegetables, but do you think that's a rule about good manners?")

5 Help them edit their spelling, grammar, and punctuation.

6 Ask children to copy each edited rule onto their book pages and to draw a corresponding illustration.

BEST-BOOK CONNECTION
The Berenstain Bears Forget Their Manners (Random House, 1990). The Berenstain Bear children learn the importance of good manners.

Follow-up Activity
Make a *Big Book of Manners* consisting of lists of manners-related rules children should follow. You might make a page for each different setting (at home, in school, in a supermarket, at a party, and so on).

Mind Your Manners

Grown-ups know a lot of rules
for eating at the table.
Here's one I try to keep in mind:

_____

Now, see if you are able.

Name _____

Gift Box

On the outside, this gift-shaped book resembles a real present. On the inside, the book pages display children's real-life gifts from the heart—and invite children to reflect on special gifts they have received and cherished. Both of these collaborative books bring new meaning to the art of gift giving.

COVER DESIGN IDEA

Cut the book cover from oak tag. Glue on real wrapping paper. Let it dry and trim to fit. Use a hot-glue gun to add a real ribbon, real bow, and gift tag, in order to complete the gift-wrapped design.

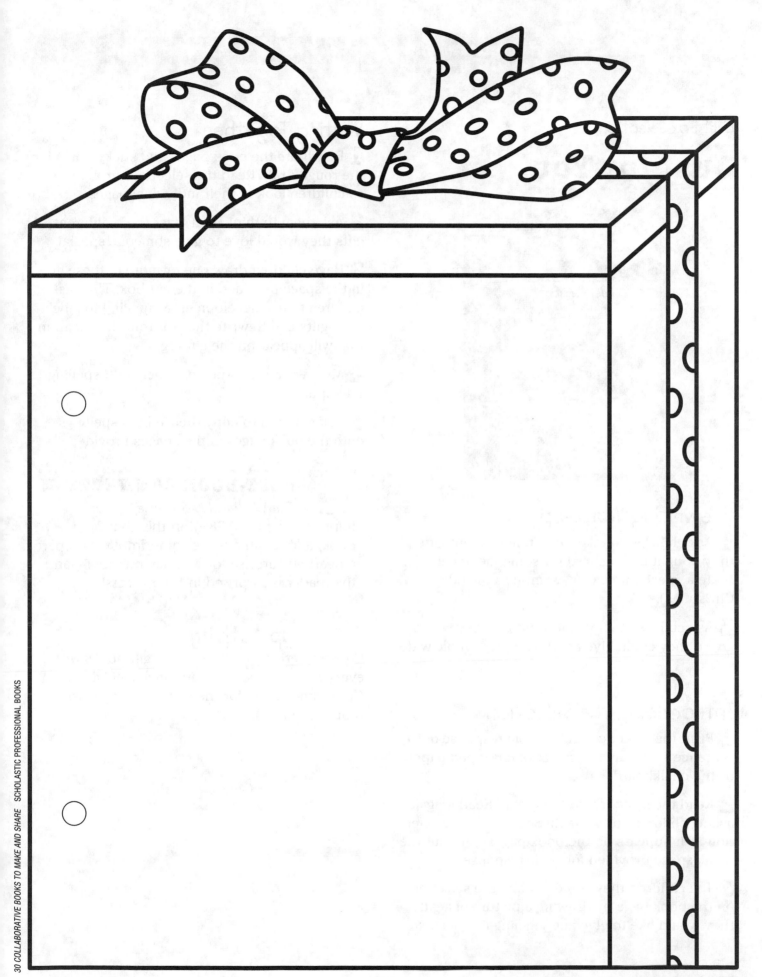

Gift Box Cover Template   **43**

Gift Box Selection A

Just for You

Just for You

Here's a gift
from me to you.
It's from my heart
with wishes true.

Surprise! It's a dog!

Prewriting Warm-up

1 Ask children to take turns telling about gifts they bought or prepared for someone to celebrate a special time (for example, a birthday, Christmas).

2 Ask children to imagine what gift they would give if they could give anything in the whole wide world.

Introducing the Selection

1 Print the selection and sample response onto sentence strips, a large sheet of chart pad paper, or the chalkboard.

2 Read the selection to the group. Read it again, asking children to chime in. Show them the selection as it appears on the book page. Point out the blank space provided for their responses.

3 Tell children they will complete the selection on the book page by drawing a picture of a gift they would like to give and labeling it.

Writing Together

1 Distribute the book pages and sticky notes for the rough draft. Read the selection through again as children look at their individual pages.

2 Ask them to think of at least three different gifts they would love to give someone special.

3 Have children draw one or more of these gifts in the space provided in the gift box. Then ask children to use developmental spelling to label their gifts and to write the "to/from" information that will appear on the gift tag.

4 Meet with each student to help edit spelling attempts.

5 Ask children to copy their edited spellings onto the book pages in the spaces provided.

 BEST-BOOK CONNECTION
The Wednesday Surprise by Eve Bunting (Clarion, 1989). In this charming book, a little girl and her grandmother prepare a heartfelt surprise for a family member—and the reader is surprised in the process!

Follow-up Activity

Create a series of collaborative gift books with every page planned for the same special person (for example, one for the principal or a classroom volunteer).

to _____

from _____

Just for You

Here's a gift
from me to you.
It's from my heart
with wishes true.

Surprise! It's _____

Gift Box Selection B

Surprise!

Prewriting Warm-up

1 Invite children to tell about the best surprise they ever received. Talk about the fact that some surprises, such as a special day or an act of kindness, cannot be placed in a box and wrapped with paper.

2 Circumstances permitting, encourage children to bring their best gifts—or a story about their best gifts—to school to share with the class.

Introducing the Selection

1 Print the selection and sample response onto sentence strips, a large sheet of chart pad paper, or the chalkboard.

2 Read the selection to the group. Read it again, asking children to chime in. Show them the selection as it appears on the book page. Point out the blank space provided for their responses.

3 Tell children they will complete the selection on the book page by providing the name of a favorite gift they received.

Writing Together

1 Distribute the book pages and sticky notes for the rough draft. Read the selection through again as children look at their individual pages.

2 Ask them to think of at least three special gifts they have received and who gave them each one.

3 Have students draw the best gift they received in the gift box.

4 Invite children to use developmental spelling to name the gift and the gift giver on the note paper provided.

5 Meet with students and encourage them to use as many specific adjectives for the gifts possible. ("Heather, you told us your Aunt Angie gave you a baby doll with brown hair, but you wrote only the word 'doll' here. Can you add some words before 'doll' to tell us more about her?")

6 Help children edit their spelling, grammar, and punctuation.

7 Ask children to copy their edited work beneath the illustration of the gift. Then they should each write their names on the gift tags after the word *to* and the gift giver's name in the space after the word *from*.

 BEST-BOOK CONNECTION
Angelina's Birthday Surprise by Katharine Holabird (Random House, 1989). Angelina the mouse is surprised when her family works together to plan a special event for her birthday.

Follow-up Activity

Make a copy of the selection. Using correction fluid, cover over the word *got* and replace it with the word *gave*. Then have children make a book of special surprises they gave to others.

to _____

from _____

Surprise!

Surprises come in every size
from big to very small.
The best surprise I ever got

was _____ .

I liked it best of all!

Name _____

Frosty Snowman

When winter winds begin to nip, here are two book ideas children will be eager to complete. Use the first frosty selection to help children imagine how they might play with a real, come-to-life snowman. Then use the second selection to have children describe the cozy indoor activities they enjoy when the snow flies.

COVER DESIGN IDEA

After cutting a snowman shape from white oak tag, cover the shape with white glue and sprinkle it with "diamond dust" glitter (available in craft and art supply stores). Referring to the cover pattern for placement ideas, add real button eyes and mouth, an orange felt carrot nose, a black felt hat, a felt scarf, and felt mittens.

Frosty Snowman Cover Template   **49**

Frosty Snowman Selection A

Snowman Alive!

Snowman Alive!

Yo, man! Snowman!
Frosty head-to-toe man!
I wish you were real, you know?
Then we could __go sledding__
here in the snow!

Name __Lee__

Prewriting Warm-up

1 If possible, begin by sharing the wordless picture book and/or the popular video version of *The Snowman* by Raymond Briggs (see Best-Book Connection).

2 After talking about what happened in the book, ask children to describe snowmen they have made. Ask them to think about what they would like to play with a snowman that has come to life.

Introducing the Selection

1 Print the selection and sample response onto sentence strips, a large sheet of chart pad paper, or the chalkboard.

2 Read the selection to the group. Read it again, asking children to chime in. Show them the selection as it appears on the book page. Point out the blank space provided for their responses.

3 Tell children they will complete the selection on the book page by providing a word telling what outdoor game they would like to play with their snowmen.

Writing Together

1 Distribute the book pages and sticky notes for the rough draft. Read the selection through again as children look at their individual pages.

2 Ask them to think of at least three different games, activities, or movements they would each enjoy playing with their magical snowmen.

3 Invite children to use developmental spelling to record one of them on the note paper.

4 Meet with students and encourage them to use the most specific language possible. ("Dakota, you say you would like to 'jump here in the snow.' Would you like to jump a special way—on one foot or up high in the snow, perhaps?")

5 Help children edit their spelling, grammar, and punctuation. Have them transfer their revised versions to their book pages.

6 Invite them to illustrate their completed selections.

BEST-BOOK CONNECTION
The Snowman by Raymond Briggs (Random House, 1978). With soft, sensuous pictures, this lovely wordless picture book tells of a magical, come-to-life snowman's adventures with a little boy.

Follow-up Activity
Invite each student to sculpt an edible snowman treat from scoops of frozen vanilla yogurt. Then decorate them with raisin eyes and mouths, candy corn noses, and scarves fashioned from dried fruit candy rolls.

Snowman Alive!

Yo, man! Snowman!
Frosty head-to-toe man!
I wish you were real, you know?

Then we could _____
here in the snow!

Name _____

Frosty Snowman Selection B

Let It Snow!

Let It Snow!

In the winter when it's snowy, icy, freezy, frosty, blowy, sometimes I stay in and play. Then I __Watch TV__ for the whole day.

Name __Luke__

Prewriting Warm-up

1 Ask children to use a show of hands to tell if they would rather play outside or inside when it snows.

2 Ask those children who would rather play inside to describe the kind of snow day that would invite them outside, too.

Introducing the Selection

1 Print the selection and sample response onto sentence strips, a large sheet of chart pad paper, or the chalkboard.

2 Read the selection to the group. Read it again, asking children to chime in. Show them the selection as it appears on the book page. Point out the blank space provided for their responses.

3 Tell children they will complete the selection on the book page by providing an indoor activity they might choose to do on an especially cold, snowy day.

Writing Together

1 Distribute the book pages and sticky notes for the rough draft. Read the selection through again as children look at their individual pages.

2 Ask them to think of at least three different indoor activities they might do on an especially cold, snowy day.

3 Invite children to use developmental spelling to record one of these activities on the note paper provided.

4 Meet with students to encourage them to be as detailed as possible about the activity they decided on. ("Matthew, I see you like to 'build with blocks.' Is there something special you like to build?")

5 Help them edit their spelling, punctuation, and grammar.

6 Ask children to copy their edited sentence ending onto their book pages.

7 Have children illustrate their selections.

BEST-BOOK CONNECTION
Something Is Going to Happen by Charlotte Zolotow (Harper, 1988). A family, sensing that something is going to happen, is delighted when they open the door first thing in the morning and gaze out onto freshly fallen snow.

Follow-up Activity

As you read aloud from a book about outdoor snow activities, such as *The Snowy Day* by Ezra Jack Keats, have children brainstorm a list of things they like to do outdoors on a snowy day.

Let It Snow!

In the winter when it's snowy,
icy, freezy, frosty, blowy,
sometimes I stay in and play.

Then I _____
for the whole day.

Name _____

Playful Penguin

Perky penguins are always a classroom favorite. In this first penguin selection, children have a chance to imagine chatting with a penguin pal. In the second selection, children can describe how they sometimes dress in fancy duds—just as penguins dress in their best black and white!

Playful Penguin

by
Ms. Martin's class

COVER DESIGN IDEA

Glue a reproducible cover pattern onto white oak tag. Trim the oak tag to fit. Use a second copy of the penguin cover as a pattern to cut felt pieces for the cover. Cover the black areas with black felt. Cover the feet and the beak with orange felt.

Playful Penguin Cover Template   **55**

Playful Penguin Selection A

If Penguins Could Talk

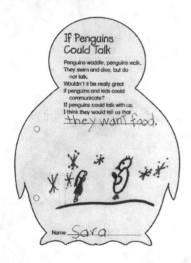

If Penguins
Could Talk

Penguins waddle, penguins walk.
They swim and dive, but do
not talk.
Wouldn't it be really great
if penguins and kids could
communicate?
If penguins could talk with us,
I think they would tell us that
they want food.

Name Sara

Prewriting Warm-up

1 Ask children how many of them take care of pets. Ask these pet owners to describe how their pets let them know when they are hungry, want attention, or are happy to see them.

2 Tell the class that the ways animals let us know what they need and want is how they communicate.

Introducing the Selection

1 Print the selection and sample response onto sentence strips, a large sheet of chart pad paper, or the chalkboard.

2 Read the selection to the group. Read it again, asking children to chime in. Show them the selection as it appears on the book page. Point out the blank space provided for their responses.

3 Tell children they will complete the selection on the book page by providing a phrase describing what they believe penguins would say if they could communicate with words.

Writing Together

1 Distribute the book pages and sticky notes for the rough draft. Read the selection through again as children look at their individual pages.

2 Ask them to think of at least three different things penguins might communicate with words, if they could.

3 Invite children to use developmental spelling to record one or more of these items on the note paper provided.

4 Meet with students to encourage them to elaborate on what penguins might say. (**Tip:** If children are stuck for ideas, show them photos and illustrations in penguin resources. These animals appear so animated it's easy to imagine them speaking when looking at their pictures.)

5 Help students polish their spelling, punctuation, and grammar. Have them transfer their revised versions to their book pages.

6 Invite them to illustrate their selections.

BEST-BOOK CONNECTION

Martha Calling by Susan Meddaugh (Houghton Mifflin, 1994). In this hilarious book, a dog named Martha is able to speak real words. Her chatty adventures will leave children wishing they could communicate this way with all animals.

Follow-up Activity

Invite children to bring in a photo or drawing of a pet they have or would like to have. Create a bulletin board featuring the animals and dialogue balloons that children fill in with words the animals might say if they could talk. (This idea works well using the class pet as a focus, too.)

If Penguins Could Talk

Penguins waddle, penguins walk.
They swim and dive—but do
   not talk.
Wouldn't it be really great
if penguins and kids could
   communicate?

If penguins could talk with us,
I think they would tell us that

_____.

Name _____

All Dressed Up

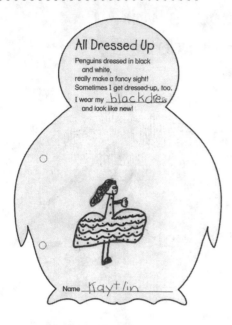

All Dressed Up
Penguins dressed in black and white,
really make a fancy sight!
Sometimes I get dressed-up, too.
I wear my _black dress_
and look like new!

Name _Kaytlin_

Prewriting Warm-up

1 Begin by showing children photos of penguin. (see Best-Book Connection).

2 Welcome comments about the appearance of the penguin. Tell children that some people think penguins look as if they are dressed in tuxedos. Invite definitions of tuxedo.

Introducing the Selection

1 Print the selection and sample response onto sentence strips, a large sheet of chart pad paper, or the chalkboard.

2 Read the selection to the group. Read it again, asking children to chime in. Show them the selection as it appears on the book page. Point out the blank space provided for their responses.

3 Tell children they will complete the selection on the book page by providing a phrase describing what they wear when they get dressed up.

Writing Together

1 Distribute the book pages and sticky notes for the rough draft. Read the selection through again as children look at their individual pages.

2 Ask them to think of at least three different words describing the clothing items they wear when dressed up.

3 Invite children to use developmental spelling to record one or more of these items on the note paper provided.

4 Meet with students to encourage them to be as detailed as possible about the clothing item(s) they decided on. ("Julie, you write that when you get dressed up you wear 'a dress.' Can you tell us a bit more about the dress? What color is it? What kind of fabric?")

5 Help children polish their spelling, punctuation, and grammar. Have them transfer their revised versions to their book pages.

6 Invite them to illustrate their selection.

BEST-BOOK CONNECTION
The Emperor Penguin's New Clothes by Janet Perlman (Penguin Books, 1994). Perky penguins are the main characters in this fresh retelling of the traditional story of "The Emperor's New Clothes."

Follow-up Activity

Plan a black-and-white penguin dress-up party in school. Have everyone dress in black and white. Serve penguin-shaped sugar cookies. (Roll out refrigerator cookie dough and cut with an egg-shaped cookie cutter; ice with white frosting and decorate with black and orange cake decorating gels to resemble penguins.) Or compile a photo album comprised of photographs of children dressed in their very best.

All Dressed Up

Penguins dressed in black
    and white
really make a fancy sight!
Sometimes I get dressed-up, too.

I wear my _____
    and look like new!

Name _____

Merry Mailbox

Beginning writers love to celebrate their letter-writing attempts! And both of these book selections give children the chance to relive that grown-up feeling they experience when they receive or send mail.

COVER DESIGN IDEA
After cutting a mailbox shape from oak tag, refer to the cover pattern and use brightly colored poster paints to paint it. Use silver paint (available in craft stores) for the top half of the box.

U.S.
MAIL

Mail for Me

Prewriting Warm-up

1 Ask children to take turns telling about real mail they received. Ask: How does it feel to get mail? What's your favorite kind of mail? Did you ever receive a package in the mail?

2 Review mail-related vocabulary such as *postcard, letter, greeting card, note, package, bill, junk mail, stamp, cancellation*. Have examples of each on hand to share, especially types children will be most likely to receive, such as a birthday card, a get-well card, a holiday greeting card, a party invitation, a travel postcard, and so on.

Presenting the Selection

1 Print the selection and sample response onto sentence strips, a large sheet of chart pad paper, or the chalkboard.

2 Read the selection to the group. Read it again, asking children to chime in. Show them the selection as it appears on the book page. Point out the blank space provided for their responses.

3 Tell children they will complete the selection on the book page by providing the name of a piece of real mail they received from someone.

Writing Together

1 Distribute the book pages and sticky notes for the rough draft. Read the selection through again as children look at their individual pages.

2 Ask them to think of at least three different pieces of mail they received.

3 Invite children to use developmental spelling to record the name of the piece of mail and the sender's name on the note paper provided.

4 Meet with students to encourage them to be as detailed as possible about the mail they decided on. ("Tamika, you wrote that you received a card from your mother. Let's think about what kind of card it was. Was it a birthday card, a get-well card?")

5 Help them edit their spelling, punctuation, and grammar. Have them transfer their revised versions to their book pages.

6 Invite them to illustrate their selections.

BEST-BOOK CONNECTION

The Jolly Postman by Janet Ahlberg (Little, Brown, 1986). The Jolly Postman has lots of letters to deliver to nursery rhyme and storybook friends. This book captivates children with its real mail tucked inside the pages.

Follow-up Activity

Invite each child to bring in a piece of real mail to share. Post the mail collage-style on a bulletin board and have children refer to the its content when creating cards and letters of their own. (**Teaching Tip:** This simple to assemble board also offers a great opportunity to do some inquiry phonics. For example, children can scan the board to locate words containing particular phonetic features, such as initial letter sounds, vowel sounds, and word endings.)

Mail for Me

I love to get real mail
from friends and family.
It makes me feel so special
when they stop and think of me.

One time, the mail carrier delivered a

_____ to me

from _____ .

Name _____

Here's What's New!

Here's What's New!

I'd like to write a letter
to show how much I care.
And then some news from over here
can travel over there.

Here's some news I would like to share in a letter:
I can do cartweels!
I would send my letter to my dad

Name Jonathan

Prewriting Warm-up

1 Ask children to take turns telling about any letter-writing experience they have had and also the many reasons we write and send letters. Perhaps children have dictated a letter to a relative, contributed to the annual family newsletter, or sent a drawing to someone they love.

2 If some children have never written a letter or contributed to a letter-writing effort, have them imagine what it would be like to send their thoughts on paper to someone they care about.

3 Remind children that everyone likes to receive mail and that their special recipient can live in the same house. (They can even send a letter to a favorite pet!)

Introducing the Selection

1 Print the selection and sample response onto sentence strips, a large sheet of chart pad paper, or the chalkboard.

2 Read the selection to the group. Read it again, asking children to chime in. Show them the selection as it appears on the book page. Point out the blank space provided for their responses.

3 Tell children they will complete the selection on the book page by providing a bit of news they would like a special someone to read.

Writing Together

1 Distribute the book pages and sticky notes for the rough draft. Read the selection through again as children look at their individual pages.

2 Ask them to think of someone they would like to send a letter to and at least three different bits of news they could write about.

3 Invite children to use developmental spelling to record on the note paper one of these news bits along with the name of the recipient.

4 Meet with students to encourage them to be as detailed as possible about their news. ("Kayla, you want to tell your dad that you are learning a lot. Let's think of something special you are learning. How about telling him you are learning to read?")

5 Help students edit their spelling, punctuation, and grammar. Have them transfer their revised versions to their book pages.

6 Have students illustrate their selections.

BEST-BOOK CONNECTION

Dear Mr. Blueberry by James Simon (McElderry Books, 1991). A clever book that showcases a series of letters between a teacher and a child regarding a whale the youngster claims is in her backyard.

Follow-up Activity

Have each child compose and polish real letters to a special someone. Arrange to take a behind-the-scenes field trip to your local post office where children can stamp and mail their letters.

Here's What's New!

I'd like to write a letter
to show how much I care.
And then some news from over here
can travel over there.

Here's some news I would like to share in a letter:

_____

I would send my letter to _____.

Name _____

Lucky Rainbow

They say that if you spot a rainbow, you'll have good luck. And children who complete these book pages will be lucky indeed! First, they'll have a chance to develop a more "color-full" vocabulary using the selection about color favorites. And then they'll have a chance to share their ideas of what they would like to find at the rainbow's end.

Lucky
Rainbow
by
Ms. Martin's
class

COVER DESIGN IDEA

Cut the cover from white oak tag. Use paints to color the rainbow. Add fluffy cotton ball clouds to both ends of the rainbow. For the second rainbow book model, *Rainbow Riches,* glue on an oak tag pot full of gold sparkles.

Lucky Rainbow Cover Template

Lucky Rainbow Selection A

Color Choice

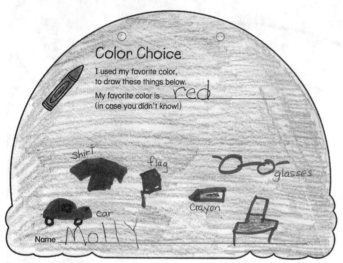

Color Choice

I used my favorite color,
to draw these things below.
My favorite color is _red_
(in case you didn't know!)

shirt
flag
glasses
car
crayon
Name _Molly_

Prewriting Warm-up

1 Ask each child to announce the name of his or her favorite color. Record these with large color-coded tally marks on a piece of chart pad paper.

2 Have on hand a large selection of paint chips (available free from home improvement or hardware stores). These are usually labeled with the name of the color. Also provide a large box of crayons in many colors labeled on the crayon wrappers.

3 Have children use plastic self-closing bags to group the paint chips and crayons according to color families (for example, the blue crayons and chips in one bag, the reds in another).

4 Read through the different color names featured on the chips and the crayons.

Introducing the Selection

1 Print the selection and sample response onto sentence strips, a large sheet of chart pad paper, or the chalkboard.

2 Read the selection to the group. Read it again, asking children to chime in. Show them the selection as it appears on the book page. Point out the blank space provided for their responses.

3 Tell children they will complete the selection on the book page by providing the name of their favorite color plus drawings done in that same color.

Writing Together

1 Distribute the book pages and sticky notes for the rough draft. Read the selection through again as children look at their individual pages.

2 Ask them to refer to the crayons and paint chips and to decide on a specific color name within their favorite color family.

3 Invite children to use developmental spelling to record one of these colors on the note paper provided.

4 Meet with students to encourage their specific color choices and rich color vocabulary. ("Wow, Jamal, I see you like an orange crayon color called 'macaroni and cheese.' That color name really tells me the shade of orange you like.")

5 Help students edit their spelling, punctuation, and grammar. Have them transfer their revised versions to their book pages.

6 Have them illustrate their completed selections with the color of their choice.

BEST-BOOK CONNECTION
My Crayons Talk by Patricia Hubbard (Henry Holt, 1996). In rhyming text, students gain insight into what colors "say."

Follow-up Activity
Have children make a crayon color poster on which they use the crayons you provided to print the detailed names of the crayon colors onto a piece of oak tag. Place the poster in your writing center.

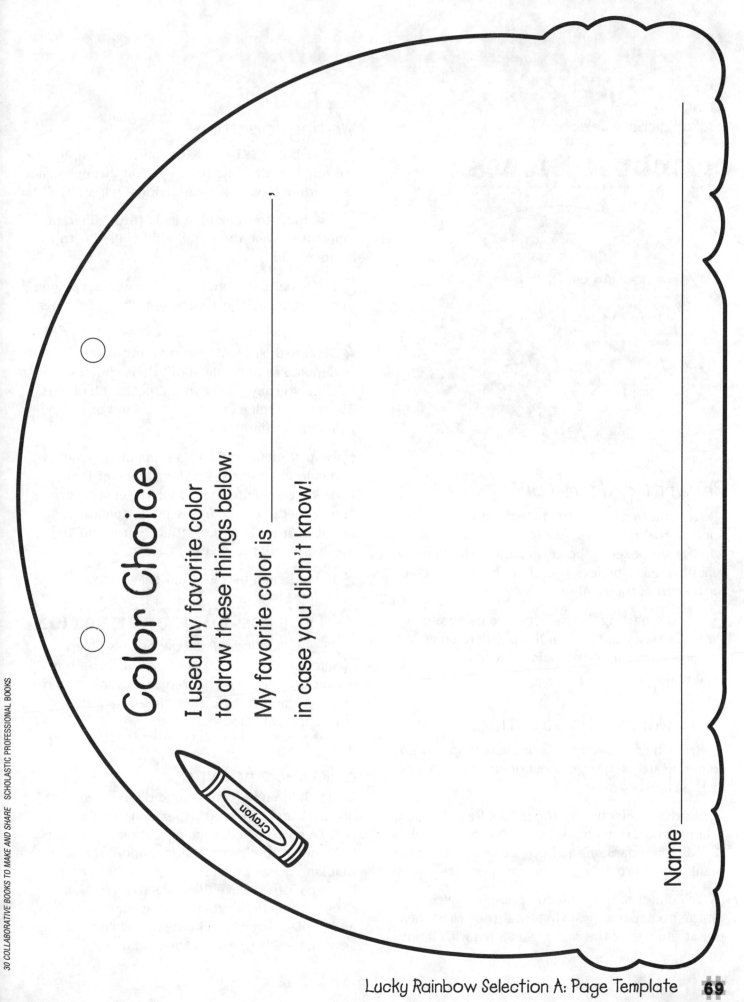

Color Choice

I used my favorite color
to draw these things below.

My favorite color is _____,
in case you didn't know!

Crayon

Name _____

Lucky Rainbow Selection B

Rainbow Riches

Rainbow Riches

They say that at the rainbow's end
A pot of gold you'll find.
But, I wish that pot was filled with
___Candies___
and that they were all mine.

Yum!

Name ___Michael___

Prewriting Warm-up

1 Ask children to tell the times and places they spotted real rainbows. Ask if any of them know what is supposed to be at the end of the rainbow. Ask how many believe that there is a pot of gold at the end of the rainbow.

2 If you are using this selection to celebrate St. Patrick's Day, ask children to speculate on why rainbows are usually associated with Irish leprechauns.

Introducing the Selection

1 Print the selection and sample response onto sentence strips, a large sheet of chart pad paper, or the chalkboard.

2 Read the selection to the group. Read it again, asking children to chime in. Show them the selection as it appears on the book page. Point out the blank space provided for their responses.

3 Tell children they will complete the selection on the book page by saying what they wish the pot at the end of the rainbow is filled with if not gold.

Writing Together

1 Distribute the book pages and sticky notes for the rough draft. Read the selection through again as children look at their individual pages.

2 Ask them to think of at least three different things they wish the pot could be filled with besides gold.

3 Invite children to use developmental spelling to record one of their wishes on the note paper provided.

4 Meet with students to encourage them to be as detailed as possible about their choices. ("Salim, you say you wish the pot is full of toys. But can you tell us exactly what kind of toys you'd like to find there?")

5 Help students polish their spelling, punctuation, and grammar. Have them transfer their revised versions to their book pages. (**Note:** The nouns children write in the blank spaces must be plural in order to agree with the pronoun *they* in the last line of the rhyme.)

6 Have them illustrate their selections.

BEST-BOOK CONNECTION
Planting a Rainbow by Lois Ehlert (Harcourt Brace Jovanovich, 1988). Use this book to introduce children to the colors of the rainbow and to help them imagine a rainbow pot filled with flowers!

Follow-up Activity

Invite children to paint a large rainbow on craft paper. From black craft paper, construct a black pot. Then, from yellow construction paper, cut "gold coins." Talk with children about the notion that kind deeds are more precious than real gold. Invite children to use the coins to record kind deeds others do for them at home and in school, and to place each coin in the pot. Hold a sharing session weekly to review the kind deeds.

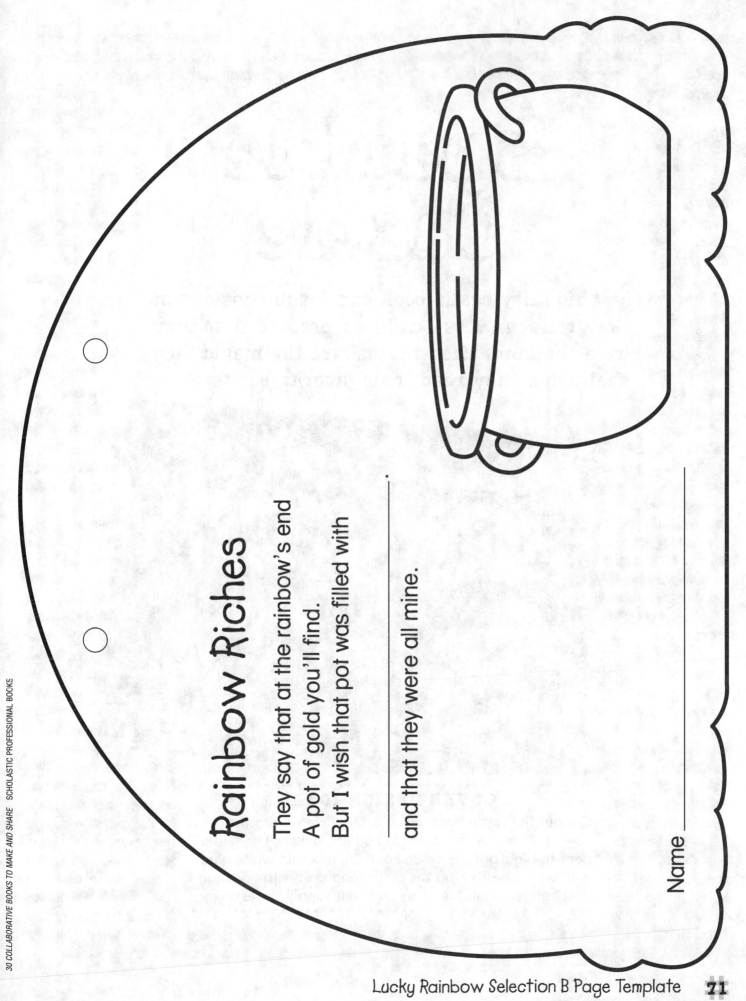

Rainbow Riches

They say that at the rainbow's end
A pot of gold you'll find.
But I wish that pot was filled with

_____

and that they were all mine.

Name _____

Sparkle Castle

This fairy castle book can inspire visions of grandeur. First, children pretend that they rule the land. Then they share the magic they feel when they read their favorite books.

COVER DESIGN IDEA

Cut out the castle from pink oak tag. Referring to the cover pattern, use a marker to add line details. Use glitter pens to highlight the castle lines. Or, mix thin white glue with water, brush it on the castle, and dust with "diamond dust" glitter (available at art and craft supply stores).

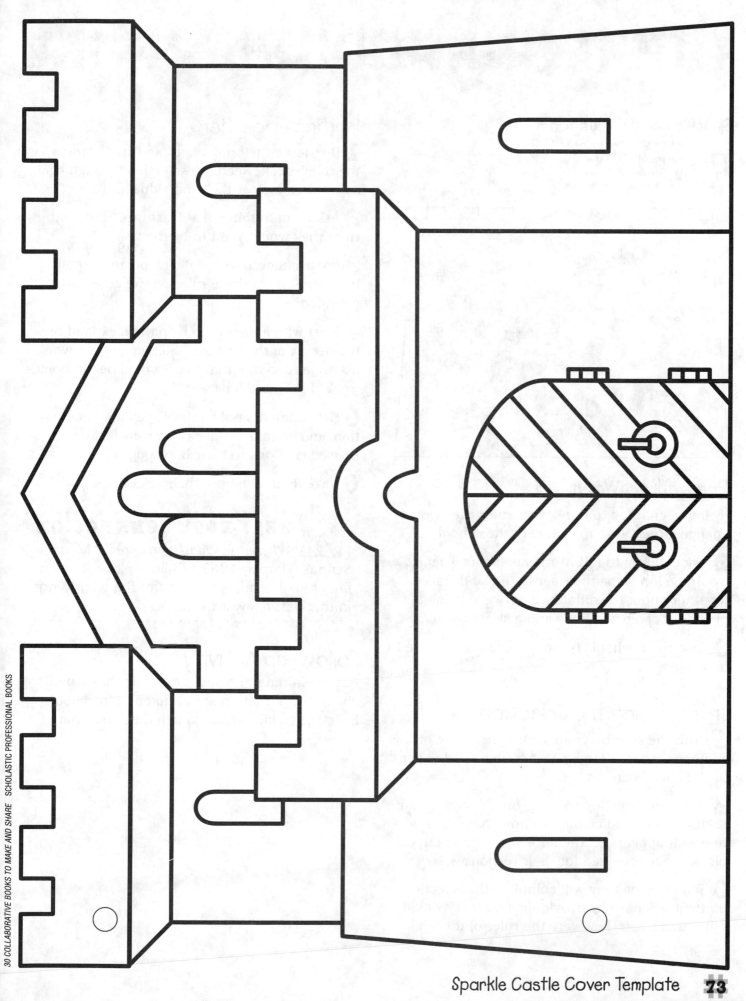

Sparkle Castle Cover Template   **73**

Sparkle Castle Selection A
Royal Rule

Royal Rule

If I were the ruler of all the land,
and lived in a castle tall,
I'd make a rule that
every person has to have a dog
and turn it into law.

Name *Paige*

Prewriting Warm-up

1 Invite children to think what rules they would change if they were in charge of the school.

2 Ask children to take turns imagining what it would be like to be the ruler of the land. Talk together about the difference between being the president of a democracy and a supreme ruler.

3 Talk about what is meant by a law as opposed to a rule.

Introducing the Selection

1 Print the selection and sample response onto sentence strips, a large sheet of chart pad paper, or the chalkboard.

2 Read the selection to the group. Read it again, asking children to chime in. Show them the selection as it appears on the book page. Point out the blank space provided for their responses.

3 Tell children they will complete the selection on the book page by providing a law they would put into place if they were the ruler of the land.

Writing Together

1 Distribute the book pages and sticky notes for the rough draft. Read the selection through again as children look at their individual pages.

2 Ask them to think of at least three different rules they would want to be the law.

3 Invite children to use developmental spelling to record one of these rules on the note paper provided.

4 Meet with students to help them expand on the details of their rules. ("So, Maeve, you would like to make a rule that there would be 'no homework.' Can you tell us why?")

5 Help students polish their spelling, punctuation, and grammar. Have them transfer their revised versions to their book pages.

6 Have them illustrate their selections.

 BEST-BOOK CONNECTION
Where the Wild Things Are by Maurice Sendak (Harper, 1963). Children love it when little Max becomes the ruler of the wild things in this classic, award-winning book.

Follow-up Activity

Have children write about one rule they would change or put into place at home or in school. Encourage children to explain their reasoning.

Royal Rule

If I were the ruler of all the land

and lived in a castle tall,

I'd make a rule that

_____

and turn it into law.

Name _____

Story Castle

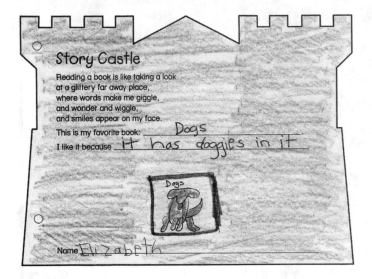

Story Castle

Reading a book is like taking a look
at a glittery far away place,
where words make me giggle,
and wonder and wiggle,
and smiles appear on my face.

This is my favorite book: _Dogs_
I like it because _It has doggies in it_

Name _Elizabeth_

Prewriting Warm-up

1 Ask children to take turns telling why they like books. Ask them if they like being read to or reading for themselves (or both!).

2 Using books from your class library as examples, have each child decide on a favorite book genre.

Introducing the Selection

1 Print the selection and sample response onto sentence strips, a large sheet of chart pad paper, or the chalkboard.

2 Read the selection to the group. Read it again, asking children to chime in. Show them the selection as it appears on the book page. Point out the blank space provided for their responses.

3 Tell children they will complete the selection on the book page by providing their favorite book titles and the reasons they like these books so much.

Writing Together

1 Distribute the book pages and sticky notes for the rough draft. Read the selection through again as children look at their individual pages.

2 Ask them to think of at least three books they especially like.

3 Invite children to use developmental spelling to record one of these book titles, and the reason for their choice, on the note paper provided.

4 Meet with students to encourage them to be as detailed as possible about the reasoning behind their book choices. ("I see here, Jane, that you like *Green Eggs and Ham* by Dr. Seuss. That's one of my favorites, too. Why do you like it? Is green your favorite color? Do you like funny books? Is Dr. Seuss your favorite author?")

5 Help students edit their spelling, punctuation, and grammar, and transfer their revised versions to their book pages.

BEST-BOOK CONNECTION

The Library by Sarah Stewart (Farrar, Straus and Giroux, 1995). Book lovers young and old will smile at this silly story about collecting piles and piles and piles of books.

Follow-up Activity

Offer children large unruled index cards and have them decorate the cards to resemble favorite book covers complete with titles. Use a pocket chart to graph their favorites according to genre (for example, realistic fiction, nonfiction, fairy tales, biography, humor, folktales).

Story Castle

Reading a book is like taking a look
at a glittery faraway place,
where words make me giggle,
and wonder and wiggle,
and smiles appear on my face.

This is my favorite book: _____

I like it because _____

Name _____

Tick-Tock Clock

Anytime is a great time to get children thinking about time. The first selection asks children to write about bedtime—or what they would do if they could stay up past their bedtimes! The second selection introduces them to the intriguing concept of relativity as it relates to time. How timely!

COVER DESIGN IDEA

Cut the clock shape from a manila folder. Add movable hands cut from black oak tag. Referring to the cover design, use a marker to add details to the front of the clock. Use brown watercolors to add a woody wash. Glue a photocopy of the clockface in place. A gold paint marker (available in art supply stores—adult use only) will add details to the wood cabinet and the rim of the clockface.

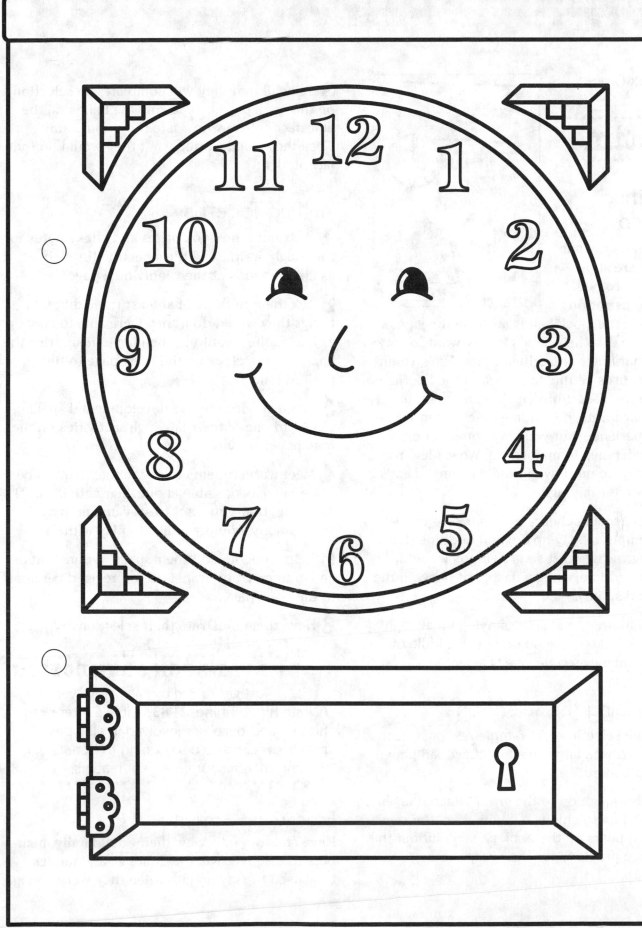

Tick-Tock Clock Cover Template

Tick-Tock Clock
Selection A

Bedtime

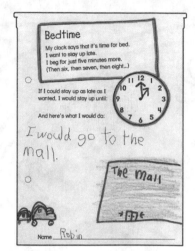

Prewriting Warm-up

1 Ask children what time they are supposed to go to bed. On a demonstration clock, place the clock hands at these times. Ask children to raise their hands if they want to stay up later than their prescribed times. Have volunteers take turns setting the clock to the bedtimes they wish for. (**Teaching Tip:** These attempts may be inaccurate, depending on children's time-telling experience, but you may comment on the times in reference to midnight. ["Wow, Meg! You want to stay up until two in the morning? That's two hours after midnight!"])

2 Consider telling children of your own childhood attempts to stay up beyond bedtime (for example, growing quiet so grown-ups would forget it was bedtime, using a flashlight beneath the covers, and so on).

3 Invite children to imagine staying up all night long. Ask: What would you do in the middle of the night when everyone else is asleep?

Introducing the Selection

1 Print the selection and sample response onto sentence strips, a large sheet of chart pad paper, or the chalkboard.

2 Read the selection to the group. Read it again, asking children to chime in. Show them the selection as it appears on the book page. Point out the blank space provided for their responses.

3 Tell children they will complete the selection on the book page by drawing the hands on the clockface to show how late they would stay up. Then they will describe what they would do that late at night.

Writing Together

1 Distribute the book pages and sticky notes for the rough draft. Read the selection through again as children look at their individual pages.

2 Ask them to think of at least three different things they would do if they were able to stay up as late as they want to. Then have them draw the hands on the clock on the book page to the desired time.

3 Invite children to use developmental spelling to record one of their late-night activities on the note paper provided.

4 Meet with students to encourage them to be as detailed as possible about their activities. ("I see, Kate, that you want to stay up and play, but what exactly would you like to play with?")

5 Help students edit their spelling, punctuation, and grammar, and transfer their revised versions to the book pages.

6 Have them illustrate their selections.

BEST-BOOK CONNECTION
Just Go To Bed by Mercer Mayer (Western Publishing, 1983). Little Critter drags his feet and becomes involved in all types of play in an effort to delay going to bed. Great reading material for emergent readers.

Follow-up Activity
Have children interview their adult family members to discover what techniques and tactics they used to stay up late when they were young.

Bedtime

My clock says that it's time for bed.
I want to stay up late.
I beg for just five minutes more.
(Then six, then seven, then eight . . .)

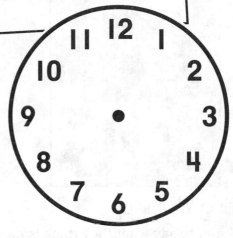

If I could stay up as late as I wanted, I would stay up until:

And here's what I would do:

Name _____

Tick-Tock Clock Selection B

Fast and Slow

Prewriting Warm-up

1 Ask children to say what they think is meant by the expression "Time flies when you're having fun." Ask them to tell about times that went by in a wink.

2 Ask students to talk about situations when time seems to drag. You can get them started with some examples of when time drags for you (for example, when you are waiting in the doctor's office, when you are standing in line at the supermarket).

Introducing the Selection

1 Print the selection and sample response onto sentence strips, a large sheet of chart pad paper, or the chalkboard.

2 Read the selection to the group. Read it again, asking children to chime in. Show them the selection as it appears on the book page. Point out the blank space provided for their responses.

3 Tell children they will complete the selection on the book page by writing about when time seems to go slowly and when it moves quickly for them.

Writing Together

1 Distribute the book pages and sticky notes for the rough draft. Read the selection through again as children look at their individual pages.

2 Ask children to think of at least three situations when time seems to move slowly and three more when it seems to move quickly for them.

3 Invite children to use developmental spelling to record one of each of these situations on the note paper provided.

4 Meet with students to encourage them to be as detailed as possible about their time-sensitive situations. ("Rhonda, I see you wrote that when you are 'shopping time never seems to pass.' Can you tell us what kind of shopping is especially boring for you?")

5 Help students polish their spelling, punctuation, and grammar, and transfer their revised versions to their book pages.

6 Have them illustrate their selections.

 BEST-BOOK CONNECTION
The Carrot Seed by Ruth Krauss (Harper, 1945). Patience and perseverance are rewarded in this simple, charming classic about a little boy who waits for his slow-going carrot seed to grow.

Follow-up Activity

Talk with children about the concept that time is relative. Ask them if they think time really travels faster when they are at an amusement park, or slower when they are stuck in traffic. Do some simple relativity experiments. For example, invite some children to play on the playground for two minutes while others spend the same two minutes sitting silently on the sidelines. Then have the groups switch places. Have children in both groups report when time seemed to pass more quickly.

Fast and Slow

Whenever I'm _____
time never seems to pass.

But whenever I'm _____
time flies by very fast.

Name _____

Beautiful Butterfly

What lovely books to complete in spring—
or even if you are just longing for spring.

COVER DESIGN IDEA

Cut a butterfly shape from pastel-colored oak tag. Decorate each wing with symmetrical designs created from glued-on sequins, glitter, and lace bits. Glue on black felt for the body and pipe cleaner antennae.

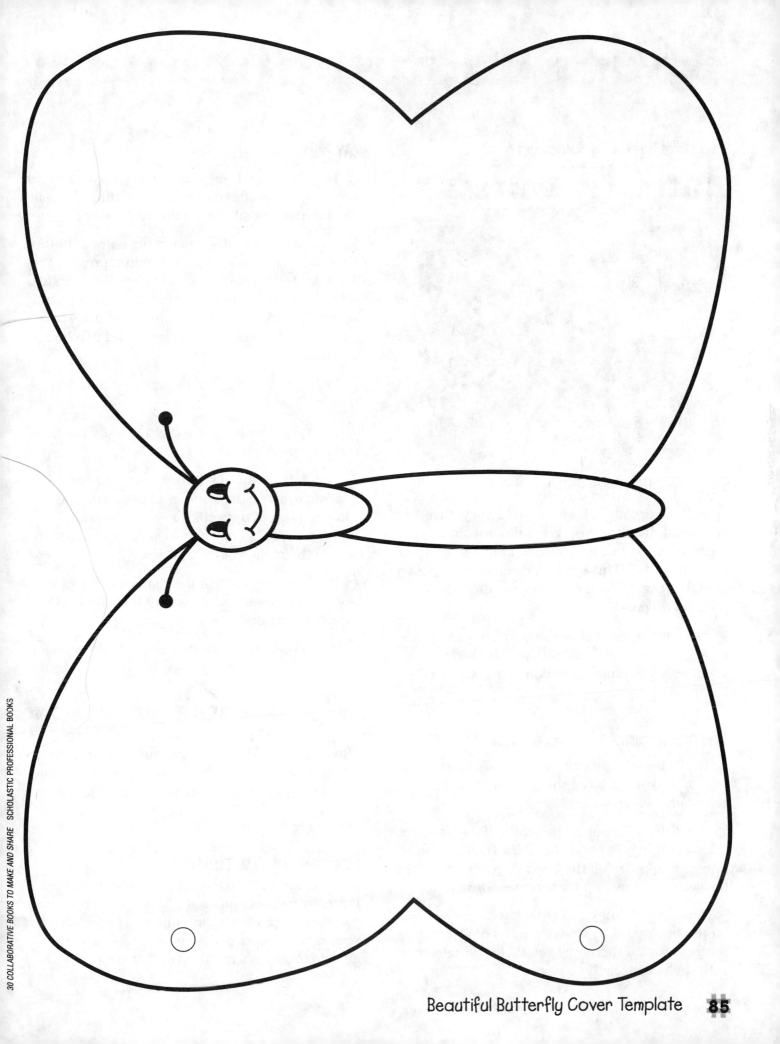

Beautiful Butterfly Cover Template   **85**

Beautiful Butterfly Selection A

Butterfly Pairs

Prewriting Warm-up

1 Ask children to tell about times they have spotted butterflies. Ask: What did you notice about how the butterfly moves in the air and when it lands? (**Tip:** Use this discussion to generate lots of butterfly movement words, such as *flutter, flit, flap, dance.*)

2 Look together at some resource materials and have children notice the different butterfly species. Invite children to comment on their favorites.

Introducing the Selection

1 Print the selection and sample response onto sentence strips, a large sheet of chart pad paper, or the chalkboard.

2 Read the selection to the group. Read it again, asking children to chime in. Show them the selection as it appears on the book page. Point out the blank space provided for their responses.

3 Tell children they will complete the selection on the book page by drawing pairs of identical butterflies, and then they will fill in the selection with the appropriate numbers.

Writing Together

1 Distribute the book pages and sticky notes for the rough draft. Read the selection through again as children look at their individual pages.

2 Ask children to draw matching pairs of butterflies on the page. Each pair should represent the same butterfly species. (For example, one child might draw two pairs consisting of four monarch butterflies, while another child might draw two pairs consisting of two monarchs and two buckeye butterflies.)

3 Invite students to circle each pair of butterflies.

4 Meet with each child to help identify the butterflies' species.

5 Encourage children to use developmental spelling to write the number of pairs and the total number of butterflies in all on the note paper provided. They may also use the paper to record the names of the species.

6 Help students polish their spelling, punctuation, and grammar, and transfer their revised versions to their book pages.

7 Invite them to illustrate their completed selections.

BEST-BOOK CONNECTION
The Butterfly Hunt by Yoshi (Picture Book Studio, 1990). This is the lush and lovely story of a child who tries to capture butterflies only to discover they are more beautiful when set free.

Follow-up Activity

Use the book shape to create construction paper butterfly puppets on craft sticks. Have students use their puppets to pantomime the playful scenes they described so others can have a chance to guess what they wrote.

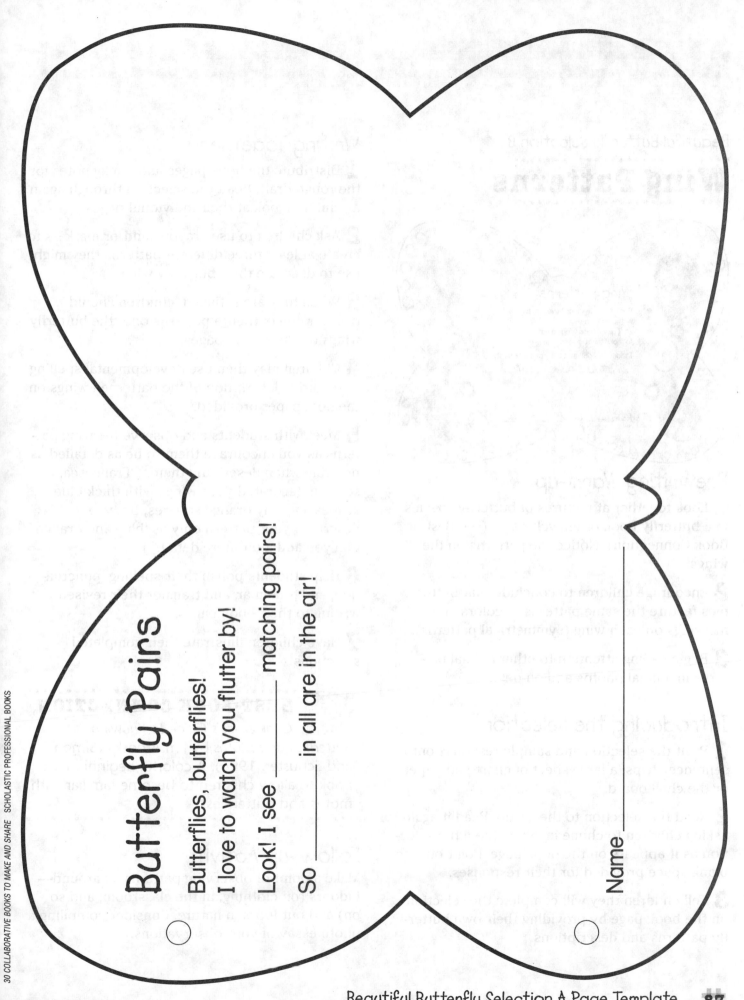

Butterfly Pairs

Butterflies, butterflies!
I love to watch you flutter by!

Look! I see _____ matching pairs!

So _____ in all are in the air!

Name _____

Beautiful Butterfly Selection B

Wing Patterns

Wing Patterns
Real butterfly wings have patterns
with colorful designs.
So I gave these wings a pattern,
to make them look so fine!
I made this pattern on my paper butterfly:
Circles and dots

Name Ellen

Prewriting Warm-up

1 Look together at pictures of butterfly species in a butterfly book or encyclopedia (see Best-Book Connection). Notice the patterns on the wings.

2 Encourage children to conclude that butterflies feature the same patterns of colors and markings on each wing (symmetrical patterns).

3 Begin calling attention to other animal patterns in animal photos and on pets.

Introducing the Selection

1 Print the selection and sample response onto sentence strips, a large sheet of chart pad paper, or the chalkboard.

2 Read the selection to the group. Read it again, asking children to chime in. Show them the selection as it appears on the book page. Point out the blank space provided for their responses.

3 Tell children they will complete the selection on the book page by providing their own butterfly patterns and descriptions.

Writing Together

1 Distribute the book pages and sticky notes for the rough draft. Read the selection through again as children look at their individual pages.

2 Ask children to use crayons and/or markers to create at least three different patterns they might use to decorate their butterfly wings.

3 When they are satisfied, children should transfer one of their a patterns onto the butterfly wings on their book pages.

4 Children may then use developmental spelling to record a description of the patterned wings on the note paper provided.

5 Meet with students and observe the wing patterns as you encourage them to be as detailed as possible when describing them. ("Francesca, I see you decorated your wings with thick blue stripes and tiny orange squares, but you described your pattern only as 'blue and orange.' Can you add a bit more detail?")

6 Help students polish their spelling, punctuation, and grammar, and transfer their revised writing to their book pages.

7 Have children illustrate their completed selections.

 BEST-BOOK CONNECTION
Crinkleroot's Guide to Knowing Butterflies and Moths by Jim Arnosky (Simon and Schuster, 1996). A colorful beginning book to allow children to become familiar with moths and butterflies.

Follow-up Activity

Make a point of observing patterns all around—indoors (on clothing, in the classroom, and so on) and outdoors in nature. Consider compiling a photo essay of your observations.

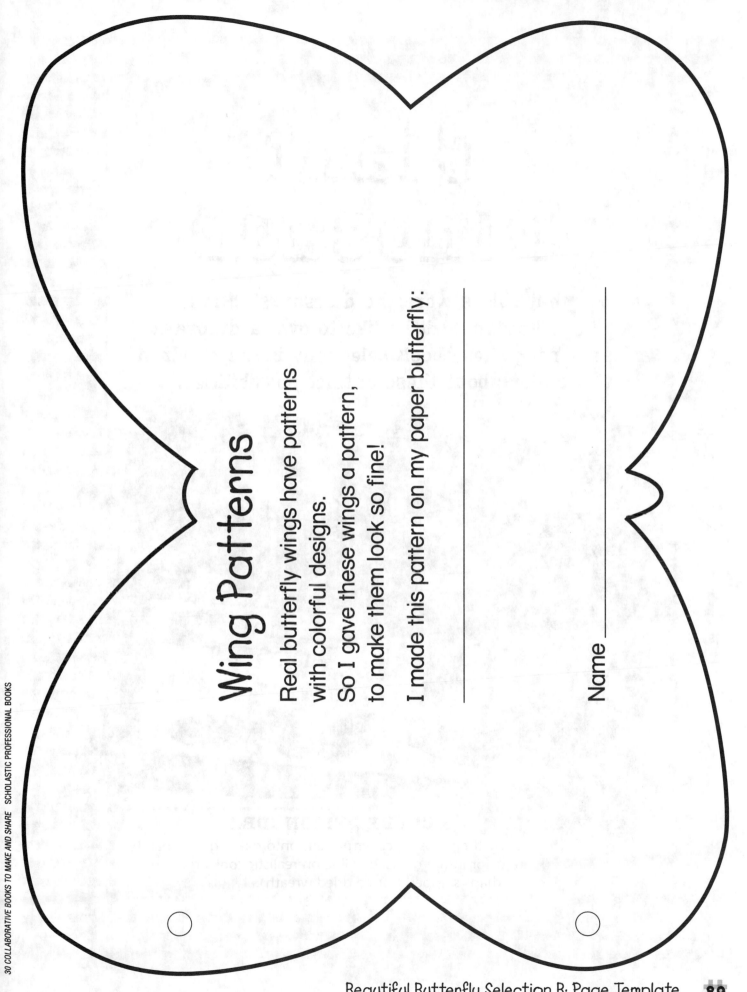

Wing Patterns

Real butterfly wings have patterns
with colorful designs.
So I gave these wings a pattern,
to make them look so fine!

I made this pattern on my paper butterfly:

_____

Name _____

Giant Dinosaur

What colors were the dinosaurs' skins? What would it be like to own a dinosaur as a pet? These book selections invite children to wonder about these extinct possibilities.

COVER DESIGN IDEA
Copy the dinosaur cover pattern onto oak tag. Use paints to color in the dinosaur. Glue on realistic-looking leaves (perhaps snipped from a dried wreath).

Giant Dinosaur Cover Template

Dinosaur Mystery

Prewriting Warm-up

1 Invite children to bring to school any dinosaur books and paraphernalia they have. Encourage them to offer information they know about dinosaurs. From your discussion, help children conclude that we know about dinosaurs because after they died their bones remained behind. Explain that even though the skin decomposed, we have impressions of the textures of skin, but the colors are a mystery.

2 Share picture books on present-day reptiles so children can become familiar with the colors and patterns featured on their skins.

Introducing the Selection

1 Print the selection and sample response onto sentence strips, a large sheet of chart pad paper, or the chalkboard.

2 Read the selection to the group. Read it again, asking children to chime in. Show them the selection as it appears on the book page. Point out the blank space provided for their responses.

3 Tell children they will each be completing the selection on their book pages by first decorating the dinosaur's skin and then describing the skin's colorings.

Writing Together

1 Distribute the book pages and sticky notes for the rough draft. Read the selection through again as children look at their individual pages.

2 Ask children to use crayons and/or markers to decorate their dinosaurs, referring to their books and other resources for inspiration. Stress that since we don't know for sure, the colorings could range from one dull-looking color to a bunch of bright colors arranged in a jazzy pattern. They should use their imaginations.

3 Children can then use developmental spelling to record a description of their dinosaur's colorings on the note paper provided.

4 Meet with students and observe the colorings, encouraging them to be as detailed as possible as they describe them. ("Emily, you used so many colors! Did you remember to include them all in your description?")

5 Help students polish their spelling, punctuation, and grammar, and transfer their revised versions to their book pages.

BEST-BOOK CONNECTION

Eyes on Nature: Reptiles by Robert Matero (Kidsbooks, 1993). Use this introduction to reptiles to offer children some ideas about what dinosaur skin may have looked like.

Follow-up Activity

Hold a "Dinosaur Day" in which children's contributions and books are displayed. Cut dinosaur-shaped sugar cookies out of refrigerator dough, ice them with tinted icing, and have children use toppings and cake gels to give these edible "dinos" some colorful "skin."

Dinosaur Mystery

I wonder about the dinosaurs' skins.
Were they gray and brown with green mixed in?
Or maybe pink and purple spotted,
Or even striped and polka-dotted!

I think dinosaur skin might have looked _____.

Name _____

Dino Pet

Prewriting Warm-up

1 Ask children to raise their hands if they have pets. Have the pet owners tell a bit about their pets, including what tricks children taught them.

2 Invite children to think about what it would be like to have a dinosaur as a pet. Consider reading *A Boy Wants a Dinosaur* by Hiawyn Oram (see Best-Book Connection).

3 Tell children that some dinosaurs were as long as two school buses and as tall as a five-story building. Others were as small as a chicken.

Introducing the Selection

1 Print the selection and sample response onto sentence strips, a large sheet of chart pad paper, or the chalkboard.

2 Read the selection to the group. Read it again, asking children to chime in. Show them the selection as it appears on the book page. Point out the blank space provided for their responses.

3 Tell children they will complete the selection on the book page by providing a word or two about what they would teach a dinosaur pet.

Writing Together

1 Distribute the book pages and sticky notes for the rough draft. Read the selection through again as children look at their individual pages.

2 Ask them to think of at least three different things they would teach a dinosaur pet. (**Teaching Tip:** Ask them to keep in mind the size of the dinosaur they want to own.)

3 Invite children to use developmental spelling to record one of these things on the note paper provided.

4 Meet with students to make certain their ideas are expanded on. ("Joshua, you say here you would teach your dinosaur pet how to 'catch,' but can you help us see your game by telling us exactly what you are throwing back and forth?")

5 Help students polish their spelling, punctuation, and grammar, and transfer their revised versions to their book pages.

6 Invite them to complete their pages by drawing pictures to accompany their passages.

BEST-BOOK CONNECTION

A Boy Wants a Dinosaur by Hiawyn Oram (Scholastic, 1990). A trip to the "dino-store" results in a real pet dinosaur for Alex.

Follow-up Activity

Encourage children to write about possibly owning other unusual pets, such as a gorilla, an elephant, or a woodpecker. (**Teaching Tip:** Stress that this is an imaginary exercise and that owning exotic pets is rarely a good idea.)

Dino Pet

I wish I owned a dinosaur.

He'd be the perfect pet.

I'd teach him how to _____

That would be fun, I bet!

Name _____

Shopping Cart

What do children want to put inside the grocery cart? What do they believe they should eat in order to grow healthy and strong? Go food shopping and find out!

COVER DESIGN IDEA

Copy the cover pattern onto oak tag. Use a craft knife to cut out the cart grid so "paper bag" pages show through. Copy book pages onto light brown construction paper and trim tops of pages with pinking shears so they resemble shopping bags. Use brass fasteners to add real oak tag wheels to front and back cover so cart can roll.

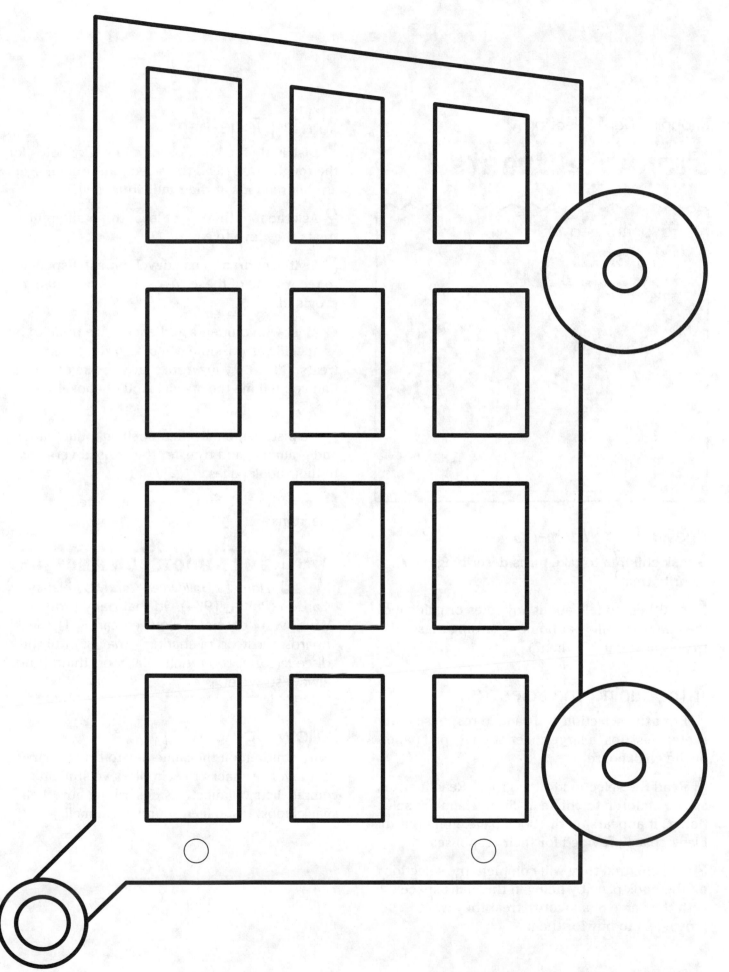

Shopping Cart Cover Template   **97**

Shopping Cart Selection A

Favorite Treats

Favorite Treats

In the supermarket
are lots of foods to pick.

But getting grown-ups to buy lolli pops
can be quite a trick.

Name Helen

Prewriting Warm-up

1 Ask children to take turns describing their favorite treats.

2 Ask them to talk about any rules or guidelines they have to follow at home regarding these treats (how much? when?).

Introducing the Selection

1 Print the selection and sample response onto sentence strips, a large sheet of chart pad paper, or the chalkboard.

2 Read the selection to the group. Read it again, asking children to chime in. Show them the selection as it appears on the book page. Point out the blank space provided for their responses.

3 Tell children they will complete the selection on the book page by filling in the blank space with the name of a favorite treat they want grown-ups to buy for them.

Writing Together

1 Distribute the book pages and sticky notes for the rough draft. Read the selection through again as children look at their individual pages.

2 Ask them to think of at least three different treats they love to eat.

3 Invite children to use developmental spelling to record one of these treats on the note paper provided.

4 Meet with students and encourage them to be as specific as possible when recording their treats. ("Tranh, you wrote that you like cookies. Can you tell me the special kind of cookie you like?")

5 Help students edit their spelling, punctuation, and grammar, and transfer the revised versions to their book pages.

6 Have them illustrate their completed selections.

 BEST-BOOK CONNECTION
Harriet's Halloween Candy by Nancy Carlson (Puffin, 1984). So that baby brother, Walt, won't eat her Halloween candy, Harriet hoards it instead of sharing—that is, until she discovers that too much of a good thing is not always so sweet.

Follow-up Activity

Invite children on the same day to bring their very favorite snacks to school. Have students compile lists of adjectives describing how their snacks look, taste, feel, sound, and smell.

Favorite Treats

In the supermarket
are lots of foods to pick.

But getting grown-ups to buy
can be quite a trick.

Name _____

Shopping Cart Selection B

Fill 'er Up!

Fill 'er Up!

First we go to the grocery store.
Next, we fill our cart.
Last, we eat the foods that feed
our muscles, bones and hearts.

My favorite healthful food is: _Fruit_ .

Name _Jaime_

Prewriting Warm-up

1 Ask children to contribute to a collaborative definition of what is meant by a "health food." Help them conclude that a health food is any food that helps our bodies grow and stay strong so they can fight off disease.

2 Together look at a Food Pyramid (located on many cereal boxes) and note the different food categories plus the recommended daily servings of each one.

3 Invite children to name their own favorite health foods.

Introducing the Selection

1 Print the selection and sample response onto sentence strips, a large sheet of chart pad paper, or the chalkboard.

2 Read the selection to the group. Read it again, asking children to chime in. Show them the selection as it appears on the book page. Point out the blank space provided for their responses.

3 Tell children they will complete the selection on the book page by providing a favorite health food or health recipe.

Writing Together

1 Distribute the book pages and sticky notes for the rough draft. Read the selection through again as children look at their individual pages.

2 Ask them to think of at least three different favorite health foods or recipes.

3 Invite children to use developmental spelling to record one of these foods or recipes on the note paper provided.

4 Meet with students and encourage them to be as specific as possible when recording their food choices. ("Colleen, you wrote that you like soup. What kind of soup is your favorite?")

5 Help children edit their spelling, punctuation, and grammar, and transfer their revised versions to their book pages.

6 Have them illustrate their completed selections.

 BEST-BOOK CONNECTION
Eating the Alphabet by Lois Ehlert (Harcourt Brace Jovanovich, 1989). This alphabet concept book offers young readers an alphabet of healthful food choices.

Follow-up Activity

Hold a "Healthful Family Food Fest" and invite families to contribute a healthful dish for everyone to sample. Compile a class recipe book featuring the recipes; make enough copies for each child to take one home.

Fill 'er Up!

First, we go to the grocery store.

Next, we fill our cart.

Last, we eat the foods that feed

our muscles, bones, and hearts.

My favorite healthful food is _____.

Name _____

Notes

Notes

Notes